Books
by
Kenneth Koch

Poems

Permanently

Ko, or A Season on Earth

Thank You and Other Poems

Bertha and Other Plays

When the Sun Tries to Go On

The Pleasures of Peace

Wishes, Lies, and Dreams:
Teaching Children to Write Poetry

A Change of Hearts:
Plays, Films, and Other Dramatic Works

Rose, Where Did You Get That Red?
Teaching Great Poetry to Children

Rose, Where Did You Get That Red?

TEACHING GREAT POETRY
TO CHILDREN

Desiree
Lynne
Collier

Do g were did you get that Bark.

Dragoon weredoyouget that flame.

kitten   weredid youget thameow

rose   weredid you getthat red.

bird weredid you get thoose wings.

Rose, Where Did You Get That Red?

TEACHING GREAT POETRY TO CHILDREN

Kenneth Koch

Random House

New York

All rights reserved under International
and Pan-American Copyright Conventions.
Published in the United States
by Random House, Inc., New York,
and simultaneously in Canada
by Random House of Canada Limited, Toronto.

Library of Congress Cataloging in Publication Data
Koch, Kenneth
Rose, where did you get that red?
1. Children's writings, American.
2. Poetry—Study and teaching.   I. Title.
PS508.C5K58   811'.5'408   72-11415
ISBN 0-394-48431-2

Manufactured in the United States of America

9 8 7 6 5 4 3 2

First Edition

Grateful acknowledgment is made for permission
to reprint the following poems:
"Oath of Friendship" from *Translations from the Chinese*
translated by Arthur Waley. Copyright 1919, 1941 by Alfred A.
Knopf, Inc., renewed 1947 by Arthur Waley. Reprinted by
permission of Alfred A. Knopf, Inc., and Constable and
Company, Inc. "Thirteen Ways of Looking at a Blackbird" from
The Collected Poems of Wallace Stevens. Copyright 1923,
renewed 1951 by Wallace Stevens. Reprinted by permission of
Alfred A. Knopf, Inc., and Faber and Faber, Ltd.
"The Wood-Weasel" from *The Collected Poems of Marianne Moore*.
Copyright 1944 and renewed 1972 by Marianne Moore. Reprinted
by permission of Macmillan Publishing Co., Inc., and Constable
and Faber Ltd. "Into the Dusk-Charged Air" from *Rivers and
Mountains* by John Ashbery. Copyright © 1962, 1963, 1964,
1966 by John Ashbery. Reprinted by permission of Holt,
Rinehart and Winston, Inc. "The Painter" by John Ashbery.
Copyright © 1956 by John Ashbery. Reprinted by permission.

To
Arlene
Ladden

Acknowledgments

Much of what is best in this book is due to Arlene Ladden, who gave a great deal of her time to helping me write and organize it. My other most important collaborators were the students at PS 61 in New York and the other children whose work is included here. At PS 61 the continuing good will of the principal, Jacob Silverman, was a great help to me, as were the interest and co-operation of the teachers I worked with there—Les Bowman, Diane Fay, and Jean Pitts. Sarah Spongberg used some of my ideas to teach children to read and write poetry at the Isidore Newman School in New Orleans and at Friends' Academy in North Dartmouth, Massachusetts, as did Mary Bowler at St. Mary's Secondary School in Swaziland. I am grateful to them for the poems they helped inspire their students to write and for the evidence they gave me that this way of teaching could work for other teachers and in other kinds of schools. Pierette Fleutiaux made it possible for me to work with her high-school students at the Lycée Français in New York. For other help and encouragement I am grateful to Pat Dreyfus, Cheri Fein, Emily Dennis Harvey, Ellen Hodge, Debby Mayer, Marilynn Meeker, Ron Padgett, James Schuyler, McKay Sundwall, Julie Whitaker, Galen Williams, and Michael Wood.

Kenneth Koch

New York City
February, 1973

Contents

Rose,
Where Did You
Get That Red?

TEACHING GREAT POETRY
TO CHILDREN

Introduction

Teaching Great Poetry
to Children

Giraffes, how did they make Carmen? Well, you see, Carmen ate the prettiest rose in the world and then just
then the great change of heaven occured and she
became the prettiest girl in the world and because I
love her.
Lions, why does your mane flame like fire of the devil?
Because I have the speed of the wind and the
strength of the earth at my command.
Oh Kiwi, why have you no wings? Because I have been
born with the despair to walk the earth without the
power of flight and am damned to do so.
Oh bird of flight, why have you been granted the power
to fly? Because I was meant to sit upon the branch
and to be with the wind.
Oh crocodile, why were you granted the power to slaughter your fellow animal? I do not answer.

Chip Wareing, 5th grade, PS 61

I

Last year at PS 61 in New York City I taught my third-
through-sixth-grade students poems by Blake, Donne, Shakespeare, Herrick, Whitman, William Carlos Williams, Wallace
Stevens, John Ashbery, and Federico García Lorca. For several years before, I had been teaching poetry writing to many
of these children, and they liked it so much that I thought
there must be a way to help them read and enjoy great poetry
by adults.

I found a way to do it, in conjunction with my students' own
writing, which enabled the children to get close to the adult
poems and to understand and enjoy them. What I did, in fact,
was to make these adult poems a part of their own writing. I
taught reading poetry and writing poetry as one subject. I
brought them together by means of "poetry ideas," which

were suggestions I would give to the children for writing poems of their own in some way like the poems they were studying. We would read the adult poem in class, discuss it, and then they would write. Afterward, they or I would read aloud the poems they had written.

When we read Blake's "The Tyger"* I asked my students to write a poem in which they were asking questions of a mysterious and beautiful creature. When we read Shakespeare's "Come Unto These Yellow Sands," I asked them to write a poem which was an invitation to a strange place full of colors and sounds. When we read Stevens's "Thirteen Ways of Looking at a Blackbird," I asked them to write a poem in which they talked about the same thing in many different ways. The problem in teaching adult poetry to children is that for them it often seems difficult and remote; the poetry ideas, by making the adult poetry to some degree part of an activity of their own, brought it closer and made it more accessible to them. The excitement of writing carried over to their reading; and the excitement of the poem they read inspired them in their writing.

I had used poetry ideas in teaching my students to write poetry before, to help them find perceptions, ideas, feelings, and new ways of saying things, and to acquaint them with some of the subjects and techniques they could bring into their poetry; I had proposed poems about wishes, dreams, colors, differences between the present and the past, poems which included a number of Spanish words, poems in which everything was a lie. I would often suggest ways of organizing the poem as well: for the Wish Poem, starting every line with "I wish"; to help them think about the difference between the present and the past, I suggested alternating line-beginnings of "I used to" and "But now"; for the Comparison Poem I suggested they put one comparison in every line, for a Color Poem the name of a color in every line. These formal suggestions were most often for some kind of repetition, which is natural

*Poems referred to in this Introduction are printed in full in the Ten Chapters.

to children's speech and much easier for them to use in expressing their feelings than metre and rhyme.

With the help of these poetry ideas, along with as free and inspirng a classroom atmosphere as I could create (I said they could make some noise, read each other's lines, walk around the room a little, and spell words as best they could, not to worry about it), and with a good deal of praise and encouragement from me and from each other, my students in grades one through six came to love writing poetry, as much as they liked drawing and painting, sometimes even more—

> The way I feel about art is nothing compared to the
> way I feel about poetry.
> Poetry has something that art doesn't have and
> that's feelings. . . .
>
> *Rafael Camacho, 6**

My poetry ideas were good ideas as long as they helped the children make discoveries and express feelings, which is what made them happy about writing—

> I like poetry because it puts me in places I like to
> be . . .
>
> *Tommy Kennedy, 6*

> You can express feelings non-feelings trees
> anything from A to Z that's why
> IT'S GREAT STUFF!
>
> *Tracy Lahab, 6*

They wrote remarkably well. Sometimes my students wrote poems without my giving them an idea, but usually they wanted one to help them get started to find new things to say.

Teaching students who were enthusiastic about poetry, good at writing it, and eager to get ideas for writing new poems, I considered the kind of poetry that they were usually taught in

---

*Here as elsewhere in this Introduction, the number following the child's name indicates the grade he or she was in when the poem was written.

school (and the way it was taught) and I felt that an opportunity was being missed. Why not introduce them to the great poetry of the present and the past? It was a logical next step in the development of their own writing: it could give them new ideas for their poems, and it would be good in other ways too. If they felt a close relationship to adult poetry now, they could go on enjoying it and learning from it for a long time.

This result seemed unlikely to be produced by the poetry children were being taught in school. The poems my students wrote were better than most of those in elementary-school textbooks. Their poems were serious, deep, honest, lyrical, and formally inventive. Those in the textbooks seemed comparatively empty and safe. They characteristically dealt with one small topic in an isolated way—clouds, teddybears, frogs, or a time of year—

> . . . Asters, deep purple,
> A grasshopper's call,
> Today it is summer,
> Tomorrow is fall.*

Nothing was connected to any serious emotion or to any complex way of looking at things. Everything was reassuring and simplified, and also rather limited and dull. And there was frequently a lot of rhyme, as much as possible, as though the children had to be entertained by its chiming at every moment. When Ron Padgett at PS 61 asked our fifth-grade students to write poems about spring, they wrote lines like these—

> Spring is sailing a boat
> Spring is a flower waking up in the morning
> Spring is like a plate falling out of a closet for joy
> Spring is like a spatter of grease . . .

> *Jeff Morley, 5*

*From "September," *The World of Language,* Book 5. Follett Educational Corp.

Jeff deserved "When daisies pied and violets blue" and "When-as the rye reach to the chin" or William Carlos Williams's "Daisy" or Robert Herrick's "To Cherry Blossoms," rather than "September." If it was autumn that was wanted, I'm sure that with a little help, he could have learned something from "Ode to the West Wind" too. There is a condescension toward children's minds and abilities in regard to poetry in almost every elementary text I've seen:

> Words are fun! . . . Some giggle like tickles, or pucker like pickles, or jingle like nickels, or tingle like prickles. And then . . . your poem is done!
> And so is my letter. But not before I wish you good luck looking through your magic window . . .*

says one author to third graders; but my third graders could write like this:

> I used to have a hat of hearts but now I have a hat
>   of tears
> I used to have a dress of buttons but now I have a
>   name of bees . . .
>
> *Ilona Baburka, 3*

I had discovered that my students were capable of enjoying and also learning from good poetry while I was teaching them writing. In one sixth-grade class I had suggested to the students a poem on the difference between the way they seemed to be to others and the way they really felt deep inside themselves. Before they wrote, I read aloud three short poems by D. H. Lawrence on the theme of secrecy and silence—"Trees in the Garden," "Nothing to Save," and "The White Horse." They liked the last one so much they asked me to read it three times:

> The youth walks up to the white horse, to put its
>   halter on

---

*"A Famous Author Speaks," *Our Language Today,* American Book Company.

and the horse looks at him in silence.
They are so silent they are in another world.

The Lawrence poems seemed to help the whole class take the subject of their poem seriously, and one girl, Amy Levy, wrote a beautiful and original poem which owed a lot to the specific influence of "The White Horse." She took from Lawrence the conception of another world coexistent with this one, which one can enter by means of secrecy and silence, and used it to write about her distance from her parents and the beauty and mystery of her own imaginings—

> We go to the beach
> I look at the sea
> My mother thinks I stare
> My father thinks I want to go in the water.
> But I have my own little world . . .*

In my new teaching my aim was to surround Amy, Ilona, Jeff, and the rest of my students with other fine poems, like Lawrence's, that were worthy of their attention and that could give them good experiences and help them in their own writing. Some of the poems would be much more difficult than "The White Horse," and all of them would probably be "too hard" for the children in some way, so I would not merely read the adult poems aloud but do all I could to make them clear and to bring the children close to them.

2

I began with the general notion of teaching my students the poems I liked best, but I soon saw that some of these were better to teach than others. Some poems came to me right away because of some element in them that I knew children would be excited by and connect with their own feelings. The fantasy situation in Blake, for example, of talking to an animal—or the more real-life situation in Williams's "This Is Just to Say" of apologizing for something you're really glad you've done. Certain tones, too—Whitman's tone of boastful secret-

*Amy's whole poem is in *Wishes, Lies, and Dreams*, p. 251.

telling. And strange, unexpected things, like Donne's comparisons of tender feelings to compasses and astronomical shifts.

Sometimes a particular detail of a poem made it seem attractive: the names of all the rivers in John Ashbery's "Into the Dusk-Charged Air"; the colors in Lorca's "Arbole, Arbole" and "Romance Sonambulo"; the animal and thing noises in Shakespeare's songs (bow-wow, ding-dong, and cock-a-doodle-dow).

Some poems had forms that suggested children's verbal games and ways children like to talk, such as the lists in Herrick's "Argument" and in Stevens's "Thirteen Ways of Looking at a Blackbird," or the series of questions in "The Tyger." Such forms would be a beginning for a poetry idea, since they were something the children could imitate easily when they wrote.

It was usually one of these appealing features that brought a poem into my mind as good to teach children. Of course, I wanted it to be a poem they could get a lot from. There are terrible poems about talking to animals and there are great ones. And the same for lists, strange comparisons, and the rest. I was looking for appealing themes and forms in the very best poems. "The Tyger," speaking to children's sense of strangeness and wonder, could heighten their awareness of nature and of their place in it. Herrick's "Argument" would help them to think about their poems in a new way, somewhat as they might think of places they had been or of specific things they had seen and done. Donne's poem could show them connections between supposedly disparate parts of their lives. Whitman could encourage them to trust their secret feelings about the world and how they were connected to it—it told them these feelings were more important than what they found in books. "Thirteen Ways of Looking at a Blackbird" showed the interest, the pleasure, and the intelligence of looking at the same thing in all kinds of ways. The Williams poems showed how poetry could be about very ordinary things. Ashbery's poem, like Donne's, could help them bring together a school subject—in this case, geography—in a playful and sensuous way with their feelings, and with poetry. One thing they could learn from them all was the importance of feelings and of one's secret imaginative life, which are so much what these poems are about. They were learning what great poetry had to do with them. Feelings they may have thought were silly or too private to be understood by anyone else were subjects that "great authors" wrote about. One reason I chose to teach Shakespeare was to show the children their connection to the poet they would be hearing about so often as the greatest who ever lived.

In deciding on poems, I wasn't put off by some of the difficulties teachers are often bothered by. Unfamiliar words and difficult syntax, for example, and allusions to unfamiliar things. My students learned new words and new conceptions in order to play a new game, or to enable them to understand science fiction in comics or on TV, so why not for poetry, which they liked just as much? Furthermore, since they were going to write poems themselves, the lesson did have something of the atmosphere of a game; and if they didn't find the poems as interesting as science fiction, I would have to figure out what was wrong with my teaching. In fact, in the excitement of reading the poems, the children were glad to learn the meanings of strange words, of old forms like *thee* and *thine,* and of strange conceptions like symmetry and sublunary.

I wasn't put off, either, by passages in a poem that I knew would remain obscure to them. To reject every poem the children would not understand in all its detail would mean eliminating too many good things. I knew they would enjoy and get something fine from Stevens's blackbird, even if the ironic allusiveness of "bawds of euphony" was going to escape them; and I was sure they would be inspired by Donne's compass even though certain details about neo-Platonism and Ptolemaic astronomy would be too hard to explain.

Though it occurred to me, at first, to reject all poems with sex or religion as part of their subject, I decided it was all right to teach poems that dealt with these subjects in certain ways.

The sexual theme in Donne's "Valediction" is implicit but not the main theme of the poem; the real emphasis is on love, the pain of parting, and the hope for reunion, all of which children can respond to. Blake's "The Tyger" is not sectarian in a way that might bother children, but touches on religious feelings of a more basic kind. Children can feel wonder and amazement and fear, and they are fascinated by superpowered beings; they can respond without difficulty to the Creator of the tyger.

Like its textural and thematic difficulties, a poem's length can make it seem impossible to teach to children. I thought if something about the poem was just right for my students, however, that it was all right to teach them only a part of it, which is what I did with "Song of Myself." I chose sections 1 and 2; in class I explained the relation of this part to the rest of the poem. There was no short poem of Whitman that I thought would teach them as much. I felt free also to select poems in another language if they had something fine in them for my students, as I thought several poems of Lorca did. I gave the children the poems in Spanish and in English translations. Translations are imperfect, and only a few children understood all the Spanish, but the good things here (the dreaminess, the music, the use of color, the contrast of original and translation itself) seemed to outweigh these disadvantages.

Rhymed poems and poems written in the lauguage of the past could have had bad effects on my students' writing, but I didn't want to omit such poems. I dealt with rhyme by showing my students the other kinds of form there were in the rhymed poem—the series of questions, for example, in "The Tyger," and the repetition of words—and suggested they use that kind of form in the poems they wrote in the lesson. Along with the rhymed poems, I included some that didn't rhyme—those by Whitman, Stevens, Williams, and Ashbery. I explained the present-day equivalents of all out-of-date words and phrases in the poems, and, while the children wrote, I urged them to use the words they really used when they spoke.

After five lessons on past poets, I did notice some conventional "literariness" in their language and in the subjects they wrote about. I didn't wish to discourage all literary imitation, since sometimes it helped the children to express genuine moods and feelings, such as awe and grandeur, which they might not have been able to express without it. However, I didn't want them to get lost in literariness. So I taught them Williams, who wrote in contemporary language about ordinary things. The example of a great poet who did this, I thought, would help the children do it for themselves.

What I saw in my students' own poetry was helpful to me in choosing poems to teach them. The extravagance of their comparisons in earlier poems ("The cat is as striped as an airplane take-off . . .") had something to do with my deciding on Donne. José Lopez's poem about talking to a dog ("Oh dog, how do you feel with so much hair around you?") was one thing that put Blake's "The Tyger" in my mind. The tone of secrecy in the poems my students wrote inspired by Shakespeare's Songs made me think of teaching Whitman and of emphasizing a tone like that in his work. In writing for the Blake lesson, some children went backwards in the history of English poetry to an earlier style of talking to nature, lamenting mortality and whimsically inquiring into origins. "Rose, where did you get that red?" and, "Oh Daffodil I hope you never die but live forever!" showed me a connection I had never thought of and showed me, too, that my students might find it interesting to read Herrick.

The usual criteria for choosing poems to teach children are mistaken, if one wants poetry to be more than a singsong sort of Muzak in the background of their elementary education. It can be so much more. These criteria are total understandability, which stunts children's poetic education by giving them nothing to understand they have not already understood; "childlikeness" of theme and treatment, which condescends to their feelings and to their intelligence; and "familiarity," which obliges them to go on reading the same inappropriate poems their parents and grandparents had to read, such as

"Thanatopsis" and "The Vision of Sir Launfal." One aspect of "childlikeness" which is particularly likely to work against children's loving poetry and taking it seriously is a cloyingly sweet and trouble-free view of life. Even Blake's "The Lamb," alone or in context with other sweet poems, could be taken that way. It is constant sweetness that is probably the main thing that makes boys, by the time they are in fifth or sixth grade, dislike poetry as something sissified and silly.

I ended up teaching, in this first series of lessons, three twentieth-century poets who wrote in English and one who wrote in Spanish; two poets who I suppose could be called Romantic —Blake and Whitman—one English, one American; two seventeenth-century poets; and Shakespeare. There was nothing of a survey about what I did. My point was to introduce my students to a variety of poetic experiences. Other teachers will doubtless want to try other poems. There are many poems children can learn from, and a teacher has a pleasantly wide choice.

3

When I became interested in teaching a particular poem, I would look for a poetry idea to go with it, such as, for the Blake class, "Imagine you are talking to a mysterious and beautiful creature and you can speak its secret language, and you can ask it anything you want." The poetry idea, as I've said, was to give the students a way to experience, while writing, some of the main ideas and feelings in the poem we were studying.

Usually one of the same features that attracted me to a poem as a good one to teach would furnish me with the start of the poetry idea. The poetry idea for Herrick's "Argument" would obviously include "Make a list of things you've written poems about"; that for Stevens would begin, "Talk about the same thing in a number of different ways." The poetry idea for Whitman would have something to do with secrets. That for Shakespeare, with noises; for Lorca, with colors; for Ashbery, with the names of rivers. The poetry idea would also have to

Venice. July 3rd 1818

1.

1.

Southey! you are a poet — Poet Laureat.
And representative of all the race —
Although 'tis true that you turned out a Tory at
Last — 'd has lately been a common case
And now — my epic Renegade!
With you — all the ~~~~ in & out of place?
A nest of tuneful persons, to my eye
"Like four and twenty Blackbirds in a pye —

2.

"Which pye being opened they began to sing"
(This old song & new Similie holds good)
"A dainty dish to set before the King"
(Or Regent who admires such kind of food)
And Coleridge too has lately taken wing,
"But like a Hawk encumbered with his hood,
Explaining Metaphysics to the Nation —
I wish he would explain his Explanation. —

3.

And Wordsworth in a rather long "Excursion"
(I think the Quarto holds five hundred pages)
Has given a sample, a new Version
Of his new System the Pages
to puzzle —

George Gordon, Lord Byron FROM Don Juan

Ricky

~~Little flower good flower~~

Mice Mice Mice Why do you
look nice? squeak squeak! Mice Mic
Mice Mice squeak squeak squeak.
Why your eyes are red? squeak. do you
sleep in a bed? Where did you get ruby
eyes? squeak squeak squeak squeak
squeak squeak mouse mouse mouseee
eeeeoeeeeeeeeeeeeeeoeeeeeeeeeeey

SQUEAK
MOUSE

The Hand-writing of John Keats.
(witness) Charles Cowden Clarke.

Give me a golden Pen and let me lean
On heaped up flowers in regions clear and calm
Bring me a tablet whiter than the psalm
Of a young Angel what time it is seen

Give me a golden Pen and let me lean
On heaped up flowers in regions clear and far
Bring me a Tablet whiter than a Star
Or hymning palm of young old angel when 't is seen
The silver things of heavenly harp atween
And let their glide by many a pearly car
And half-seen wings, and glances keen
Plush Robes and diamond hair
The while let Music wander round my ears
And as it reaches each delicious ending
Let me write down a Line of glorious tone
And full of many wonders of the Spheres—
For what a height my Spirit is contending
'Tis not content so soon to be alone—

John Keats Sonnet XII

fear.   Vilm

I
feared
my
shadow
but
It
was
nice
to
see
my
self
in
fear.

Ah, not ~~that~~ granite dead and (latest) cold!

Ah, not ~~that~~ granite dead and cold!
Far, far from base and shaft expanding — the
~~limited~~ round zones circling, comprehending,
No lurid fame exceptional, ~~for~~ ~~mentions~~ in-
tellect nor conquest's domination ~~in entire~~
Thou Washington art all the world's — not
yours alone, America
Europe's as well, in every ~~but~~ castle of lord, or laborer's cot —
Or from the Arab's in his tent — the African's,
Old Asia's there with venerable smile seated
amid her ruins,
Great the antique the hero new? 'tis but the
same — the indomitable heart and warm — the
heir legitimate — ~~the same~~ ~~of the never broken line~~
Courage, alertness, patience, hope, the same — e'en
in defeat defeated not the same;)
Where'er ship sails by, or house is built on land,
or night or day,
Through teeming cities' streets, indoors or out,
factories or farms,
Now, or to come, or past — wherever patriot
wills existed or exist
Wherever Freedom, poised by Toleration, swayed
by Law, — ~~in them, from them,~~
~~Rising or risen there's thy true monument,~~
Rises or is rising thy true monument,
stands

Walt Whitman FROM *Ode to Washington*

① Gravity

love is like gravity pulling adeversed
cupple together. because whenure
seperate we are pulled together
aging

②   mornin dew

love is like a soft mornin dew
which has a magic formula which makes
love appere

③   courgive and fourget

④   Love = 2 planets joining to make
       a eclips

     Love = a rocket ship going to the
     moon when the astrohaut sees
     venus the capsule goes crazy and
     hits venuses shade and what
     a ugly venas the the ship takes off

connect the poem to the children's feelings and include
suggestions for a form in which they would enjoy writing. So
I would work out and elaborate my first conception for a poetry idea until I could give it to the children in a way that
would immediately make it interesting and make them eager
to write.

Some poems presented no problem . Once the children saw
what they were about, they were eager to write poems like
them of their own. This was the case with "This Is Just to Say."
Apologizing for something they were secretly glad they had
done was so familiar and amusing an experience that in order
to inspire them to write about it I had only to show them what
the poem was about. Ashbery's river poem had an equally
obvious and immediate appeal just as it was, a poem with a
different river in every line. In this case, however, I was a little
afraid of a merely mechanical response, so I said "Write a
poem with a river in every line, and really imagine you are
seeing the river or are floating on it, and say how it really looks
and feels. If you want to, put in colors and sounds and times
of year. Think what color each river is, what kind of sound it
makes, what month of the year it reminds you of." Ashbery's
poem doesn't include such details about each river, but thinking about such details helped the children go from one real,
sensuous experience of a river to another—"Delaware—green
with April birds and flowers/Missouri—red January bugs and
laughter. . . ." *(Mayra Morales, 5).*

Herrick's poem, like Ashbery's, had something immediately
appealing for the children to imitate: a list of subjects they
had written poems about. However, to enjoy making such a
list, as Herrick evidently did, a child would have to be in a
similarly pleasantly expansive and satisfied state of mind. I
could help to make children feel this way by reminding them
of the poems they had written for me about colors, noises,
wishes, lies, and dreams. I could suggest they think, too, of
their poems in more detail. Had they written, as Herrick says
he has, of flowers? of girls? of love? of things to eat and drink?
That was good as far as it went, but some of the children had

written only a very few poems. To help them out, and to give
to everyone's poem more of the impetus of pleasure and
desire, I made it part of the poetry idea that, along with writing of what they had already written about, they could say
what they would like to write about in the future. This makes
the poem more exciting.

Williams's "Between Walls" had an appealing idea—something supposed to be ugly which really is beautiful—but the
children would get more out of it if I could connect it to their
feelings as well. I did that by using the words *really* and *secretly,* which I found as helpful here as, in other lessons, appealing to the children's senses and asking them to think of
colors and sounds. My suggestion was, "Write a poem about
something that is supposed to be ugly, but which you *really
secretly* think is beautiful, as Williams thinks the broken glass
shining in back of the hospital is beautiful." Another time
secret was a help was in the Blake class, when, to make the
children believe more in the reality of the situation (their
talking to an animal or other creature), I said that they should
pretend they could speak its secret language.

I saw right away that Shakespeare's "Come Unto These Yellow Sands" was attractive to children for its gaiety and for its
use of sounds, but I didn't find a way to connect it to their
feelings until I began to think about its being an invitation and
how exciting the situations of inviting and being invited are
for children. Invitations are connected with birthdays and all
sorts of mysteries and surprises. My poetry idea, which helped
the children get the genuine strangeness of this and other
Shakespearean songs, was to write a poem inviting people to
a strange and beautiful place, full of wonderful sounds.

Sometimes my students' reactions would lead me to change
the poetry idea. In the Blake class my poetry idea was to ask
a creature questions. Several children asked me if they could
put in the answers, too. I said yes. Though including answers
would make a poem less like Blake's on the surface, it could
make it more like his in a more important way if it helped the
child believe in the human/animal conversation. Conversa-

tions are easier to believe in if someone answers. Another question in the Blake class was "Can we talk to a different creature in every line?" I agreed to this, too. It would make the poem easier for those children who that day didn't feel up to sustaining a whole poem about one animal, bird, or insect and might help them refresh their inspiration in every line. And Blake himself had addressed a number of different creatures in *Songs of Innocence and Experience.*

These variations of the poetry ideas weren't false to the poems except in insignificant ways. I didn't want a poetry idea which commanded a child to closely imitate an adult poem. That would be pointless. I wanted my students to find and to re-create in themselves the main feelings of the adult poems. For this purpose, a lot of freedom in the poetry idea was necessary. They would need to be free, too, from demands of rhyme and metre, which at their age are restrictions on the imagination; and from the kinds of tone and subject matter which might oppress them. In relation to "The Tyger," this meant suggesting they write a poem in the form of repeated questions rather than asking for five stanzas of couplet-rhymed tetrameter; and that they write about talking to a strange creature, rather than that they write about The Wonders of God's Creation.

I could be fairly sure I had a good poetry idea worked out when examples of lines to illustrate it came easily to me. If I could think of lines inviting people to strange places or of ugly things that are really beautiful or of comparisons between geometry and magnetism and how I felt about someone, the children, with my help, would be able to as well. The final test of the idea, though, would be in class—if my suggestions for a poem weren't exciting and clear to the children, then I would have to find a way to make them so.

There are, of course, different writing suggestions, different poetry ideas that one can use with a particular poem. I approached the wonder and amazement in Blake through the theme of talking to an animal. My own childhood had been colored by the fantastic hope that I would be able to speak to animals and birds and share my feelings with them and find out their secrets, and this was one thing that made me feel my students might respond well to this particular idea. But I could just as well have approached the wonder and amazement through the theme of origins, of thinking of all the strange things in the world and imagining how they were made. Or by the theme of marveling at the superpowered being who does everything that is done in the world. In such a poem, for example, each line might begin with, "Who would dare . . . ?" and the children could be helped to begin by a few examples like "Who would dare to make a tiger?": Who would dare to lift the red-hot sun out of the street every morning? Who would dare to push the electricity through the subway tracks? Who would dare to go out into the middle of the ocean and push the waves to shore?

Writing suggestions have been used with teaching poetry before. Those I have seen in textbooks, however, are unhelpful either because they don't give the child enough (Write a Poem of Your Own about a Tiger), or bad because they give him too much—often, for example, telling him what to feel—(Write a Poem about How Beautiful You Think Some Animal Is). "Write a Poem in Which You Imagine Talking to an Animal" is in the right direction, but not dramatic enough. A writing suggestion should help a child to feel excited and to think of things he wants to write.

4

I would go to my classes at PS 61 with copies of poems for everyone. I would pass them out and ask the children to read them. I would tell the children that I would explain what was unclear to them in the poetry and that after we had discussed it they would write poems of their own that were like it in some way. Interested, as they always were, in anything connected with their writing, my students read the work to themselves, then listened to me read it aloud, and our discussion began.

When I talked about the poems, I tried to make the children feel close to them in every way I could. The fact that they were going to write a poem connected to the one we studied was a start. Beyond that, I wanted to make the poem as understandable as possible, and also as real, tangible, and dramatic as I could. I wanted to create excitement about it there in the classroom. When I could judge from what the children said and from their mood in general that they had understood the poem and its connection to themselves and to things they wanted to say themselves, I would have them write.

Many details of adult poetry are difficult for children, but they are glad to have them explained if they are interested in the poem, and if they aren't made to feel that the poem is over their heads. I immediately made the dramatic situation of the poem clear, often by a few questions. Who is Blake talking to? Why does he think that the tiger is "burning"? I responded in a positive way to all their answers; even wrong answers would show them thinking about the poem and using their ingenuity, trying to understand. Once started on that path, with my help and that of their classmates, they eventually understood. As soon as I could, I would begin to associate the poem with their own experience. Have you ever talked with a cat or a dog? Have you ever seen its eyes in the dark? Did they shine like those of the tiger? Unfamiliar words, such as *fearful* and *frame,* and odd syntactical constructions, such as "What dread hand? and what dread feet?" I treated as small impediments in the way of enjoying the big experience of the poem, to be dealt with as quickly as possible. I explained them briefly and went on.

Along with doing all I could to make the poem available and easy, I did things in every class to dramatize the poem and make the children excited about it. When we came to Blake's lines about the creation of the tiger's heart, "And what shoulder, and what art / Could twist the sinews of thy heart?" I asked the children to close their eyes, be quiet, put their fingers in their ears, and listen hard: that strange, muffled thumping they heard was their heart—how must Blake have felt imagining the tiger's heart, which was probably even stranger? To dramatize Donne's compass image and show the children how it really worked, I brought a big compass to school and showed them what his comparison was about in every detail. In the Lorca class, to help them feel the music and the magical use of colors, I had the children close their eyes and listen while I said words in English and in Spanish, such as "green" and *"verde,"* and asked questions such as "Which word is greener? Which is brighter?" To excite the children about Williams's "The Locust Tree in Flower," I began by having the whole class write a poem like it together, the children shouting out lines to me, which I wrote on the blackboard. In the Ashbery class I had the children call out to me the names of all the rivers they could think of. In the Herrick class, they named the things they had written about and the things they wanted to write about.

The discussion of some poems went more quickly than that of others. The discussion of the Williams poems, for example, was very brief. After a few readings and a few questions, the children seemed really to have a sense of the poems and to be ready to write. They were starting their own poems five minutes after the class began. I spent a good deal more time discussing "The Tyger." I wanted to be sure to communicate to the children the main feelings in the poem—fear, amazement, and wonder—which seemed less accessible to them than the main feelings in "Between Walls" and "This Is Just to Say." It seemed good to linger over particular parts of the poem to make them dramatic and real—the tiger's burning, the forests of the night, the fire in the tiger's eyes, the making of the tiger's brain in a furnace. Even my explanation of *symmetry,* a word none of my students knew, helped to involve them in the poem. I showed them that they themselves were symmetrical, and—excitedly touching their own shoulders, elbows, ears, and knees—they could feel the strangeness of the tiger's symmetry, too. I didn't think it necessary to teach every detail of a poem, just those that would help give the children a true sense of its main feelings.

Once they had that sense, I would give them the poetry idea; sometimes I would have given them a suggestion of it earlier in the lesson, so they could think about it while going over the poem. Now I had to make sure that it was clear enough to help them write a poem. First I would explain the idea, then answer questions about it; then give the children a few examples of how it would work out, what kinds of subjects they might deal with, what kinds of lines they might write. When I had suggested a few possibilities, like, "You can compare you and your girlfriend or boyfriend to magnets," or "You can ask questions like 'Lion, where did your terrible roar come from?' " I would ask the children for ideas and sample lines of their own. When these came to them easily, and when a lot of hands were raised in the air to give me more and more of them, that is, when the children were obviously understanding the project and full of ideas, I would pass out paper and they would write.

This writing part of the lesson was the same as it had been in my classes on teaching poetry writing alone, without adult poetry. The children talked, laughed, looked at each other's poems, called me to their desk to read and to admire, or, if they were "stuck," to give them ideas. It was a happy, competitive, creative atmosphere, and I was there to praise them, encourage them, and inspire them. When a student finished a poem quickly, I would sometimes suggest he write another. Some sixth graders were so excited about Williams's "This Is Just to Say" that they rapidly wrote three or four poems, apologizing to their dog, their fish, their parents, and their friends—to the dog, perhaps, for eating its biscuit, to the fish for forgetting to feed it, to their mother for breaking a dish, to a friend for eating the flowers off his head. In the Lorca class, if they had finished quickly, I asked those children who had written their poems all in Spanish to take another sheet of paper and write a translation. Sometimes when a child felt seriously impeded, I'd suggest he write a poem in collaboration with somebody else, or I would write one with him myself, which is how Rosa

Rosario and I wrote "Poem: At six o'clock. . . ." My aim in general was to move around enough and respond enough to what the children were writing to keep things going happily all over the room.

I wanted to keep the free and pleasant atmosphere my students had always had in which to write poetry. There was no reason why the presence of great poems should interfere with that. I did everything I could in our discussion to make the poem seem easy and familiar to them. Now, while they wrote, I let the poetry idea take over from the adult poem, and their own ideas lead them in various directions. In the Blake class: Yes, you can talk to a stone if you wish, instead of an animal. Yes, Markus, you can write it in "octopus language." Yes, you can, instead of asking the animal questions, tell it what to do. I would stress, all the while, the part of it I thought would most inspire them: But remember, whatever you do, that you are really talking to it—really. I said yes, too, to my Spanish-speaking students, in the Lorca class, who wanted to write their whole poems in Spanish instead of just using Spanish words for colors. And to Yuk, a Chinese girl in the same fifth-grade class, who asked if, instead of Spanish words, she could use Chinese color words in her poem. When I praised the children's lines, it was not for their resemblance to Blake or to Donne, but for what they were in themselves—sometimes very much like the work of the poet we started with and sometimes less so—

> Giraffe! Giraffe!
> What kicky, sticky legs you've got.
> What a long neck you've got. It looks like a stick of
> fire. . . .
>
> *Hipolito Rivera, 6*

The adult poem started them off, but this part was all their own, and had to be, otherwise the lesson would come to nothing. Forced imitation could make them hate the adult poem rather than like it and wouldn't bring them close to it. But the energy and volatility of their imagination were a different kind of educational force. Anything the poem started in their imagination, and wherever it took them, I thought was fine.

To help them be free as they wrote, I urged them to write mainly in their own language, rather than in that of the poem, if it was from an earlier time. Rhyme, as I have said, I told them they needn't use. And, as in all my poetry classes, I asked them not to worry about spelling (or punctuation or neatness). All that could be corrected later. De-emphasizing these mechanical aspects of writing makes it easier for everyone to write and makes it possible thereby for some children who would not otherwise have dared to write poetry to write it and to come to love it; I had children like this, in fact, terrible spellers, who developed into fine and enthusiastic poets, and into students with more confidence in themselves as well.

The children usually wrote for about fifteen minutes. I tried to give everybody time to finish, though if one or two children were still writing after everyone else was waiting to give me his poem, I collected all but theirs and let them go on writing. Sometimes I would read the poems aloud to the class. More often the children would read them themselves—they had come to enjoy doing that quite a lot. Afterward I would mimeograph their poems and include among them the adult work we had studied. Blake's "The Tyger" woud be there between Loraine Fedison's "Oh Ants Oh Ants" and Hipolito Rivera's "Giraffe! Giraffe!" and, I felt pretty sure, somewhere in everyone's memory and imagination as a real and vivid experience.

To help children write well and enjoy it, perhaps the most important thing to do, I found, is to be positive about everything. I responded appreciatively to what they said and to what they wrote. Everything had some value, the very fact they could imagine talking to an animal, anything at all they found to say to it. So encouraged, they could go on to do more. Poetry writing is a talent that thrives, in children at any rate, on responsiveness and praise. If I preferred some lines or ideas to others, I responded more enthusiastically to those, rather than criticizing the ones I liked less.

5

I was assured the children were learning something by their continuing interest in class and by the poems they wrote. Sometimes a child wrote a poem that showed a remarkable mastery of a particular poet's way of seeing and experiencing things—

Goldglass

In the back yard
Lies in the sun
White glass
Reflecting the sun

Marion Mackles, 6

Marion's poem, written in a class on William Carlos Williams, shows not only Williams's attention to the beauty of small and supposedly unbeautiful things, but also his way of making the poem, as it goes along, a physical experience of discovery for the reader. Sometimes what the children wrote would be in many ways unlike the adult poetry we read, yet obviously inspired by it, as were a number of poems written in the Shakespeare class, poems about escaping into freedom: free-dom from school; freedom from the powerlessness of child-hood; freedom, even, from ordinary reality—

Oh come with me to see a Daisy. . . .
And put a lion on the chair and let teacher sit on it . . .
. . . and let her give no homework for the rest of the
    year . . .

Andrea Dockery, 5

We'll fly away, over mountains and hills.
And then for us the world will stand still.
The world will be at our command . . .

Maria Gutierrez, 5

> We are free, free, come, come, I am inviting you to
> the land of freedom where dogs go quack quack
> instead of bow, wow, bark, bark. . . .
>
> *Rosa Rosario, 5*

Of course, I didn't give quizzes or tests of any kind on poetry.
A few bad marks would have made poetry, for most of my
students, an enemy. But though few had the critical skill to say
much about the poems we read, they all could experience
them. For the space of reading the Blake poems and writing
Blake-like poems of their own, the children were confronting
tigers; they were talking to nature; they were lifted out of their
ordinary selves by the magic of what they were saying; the
fresh power of their feelings and perceptions was, for a moment, a real power in the world. One may feel, as a poet I know
said to me, that "some things should be saved for later." Some
things inevitably will be, because there are aspects of Blake's
"The Tyger" and Donne's "Valediction" which elementary-
school children won't respond to. But to save the whole poems
for later means that some important things will be lost, permanently—the experience, for example, of responding to
Blake's poem when one is ten years old and can still half
believe that one's girlfriend was created by a magical transformation and that one can talk to a lion about its speed and
its strength; or the experience of "Come Unto These Yellow
Sands," when one can believe in the magic of dancing oneself
into oneness with nature; or reading John Donne when rocketry and desire can be thought of together in an unaffected way.

All these are good experiences to have. When a child has
had a few of them, he may begin to anticipate finding more of
them in poetry and want to read more of it, rather than being
cut off from it, as so many schoolchildren now are. My students, of course, were also being helped as writers. The adult
poems added good things to their own work. When they picked
up their pencils to write now, there were a few more tones
they could take, more ways to organize a poem, new kinds of
subject matter they could bring in.

6

Different children did their best work at different times. A few young poets suddenly came to me in the class on William Carlos Williams's "This Is Just to Say"; I suspect it was the naughtiness theme (apologizing but really glad) that did it. Some Spanish-speaking students wrote their best work in the Lorca class, obviously delighted at the chance to read a poem in school in their language and to be able to use Spanish in their own poems. Some classes were altogether better than others. The children's responses to Blake and Donne were especially strong and convincing, whereas I felt my students had not gotten as much as they might have from Stevens. I thought of a better way to teach Stevens only afterward.* Sometimes even with the best of poems and poetry ideas, a poetry class would go badly; the children would be tired or out of sorts, or I would be, and the enthusiasm and excitement conducive to writing poems wouldn't be there. Sometimes a lesson picked up suddenly after a good idea that some student or I had; at other times it seemed best to put off poetry till the next day. In any case, a dull class doesn't mean that children "aren't really interested" in poetry, but only that something is interfering with their feeling that interest as strongly as they might.

The differences between grades were like those I had already noticed in teaching writing. Third- and fourth-graders tended to be more exuberant, bouncy, and buoyant than their more serious older schoolmates. One of their characteristic reactions was to write "joke poems," which made fun of some aspect of the poem or of my poetry idea—of talking to an animal in its secret language, for example, in the lesson on Blake—"Glub blub, little squid. Glub blub, why blub do you glub have blub glubblub blub such glub inky stuff blubbb? . . ." (Markus Niebanck) or in the same lesson, of

*Some of these late thoughts are in the Stevens chapter. Usually when I had ideas for improving a lesson, I'd have a chance to try it again. Often, when I taught two or three different classes (of different children) in succession, the later ones would profit from what I'd learned in the earlier.

the strangeness of creatures—"Little duck, little duck, how did you get those iron legs? / How did you get those steel eyes? . . ." (Edgar Guadeloupe). These were fine responses to the poems and I showed my appreciation of them. Wildness and craziness and silliness were means for all my students to make contact with their own imaginations and through them with the adult poems, and they were especially important to the seven-to-nine-year-olds. The fifth- and sixth-graders were usually somewhat more responsive to the texture and detail of the poems, or at least better able to transfer certain qualities of phrasing and tone to their own work, as in these lines from the sixth-grade Blake poems: "Oh butterfly oh butterfly / Where did you get your burning red wings? . . ." (Lisa Smalley), "When the stars fall to the earth and the purple moon comes out no more . . ." (Andrew Vecchione). Third- and fourth-graders, however, showed they were quite able to get the essentials: "Oh, you must come from a hairy god! . . ." (from "Monkey" by Michelle Woods); ". . . Ant, the most precious, where did you get your body? / Beautiful butterfly, where did you get your wings? . . ." (Arlene Wong).

One thing I think all of my classes profited from was the fact that the children had written a number of their own poems before, independently of the study of the adult works. Some had as many as twenty classes in writing poetry, some only five or six. All had enough to make them feel like poets, however, and this was a great help to them in reading what other poets had written. They were close to poetry because it was something they created themselves. Adult poetry wasn't so strange to them; they could come to it to some degree as equals. A good teacher can bring poetry close to children anyway, but their already feeling easy and happy about it is a real advantage. When they took up their pencils to write works inspired by Blake, Donne, and the other poets, they already knew what it was like to write poetry. They had experience of using comparisons, noises, colors, dream materials, wishes, lies and so on. This gave them a better chance to create something original in the presence of the adult poems, which might otherwise have been simply too intimidating. I suggest beginning the teaching of poetry with writing alone; then, after five or six lessons, introducing such adult poems as the children seem ready for. In these first classes a teacher can get a sense of what children like about poetry and how best to help them to write and to enjoy it.

In the first few lessons using adult poetry, it may be good to bring it in mainly simply as an inspiration for the children's own work—that is, not discussing the adult poem at all, but merely using it as an example—as I did with the poems by Lawrence and Ashbery. In this way the children can get accustomed to a free and easy relationship with it. One may decide, too, to alternate the classes using adult poetry with some sessions of only writing. The important thing is to keep the atmosphere free, airy, and creative, never weighed down by the adult poems. Once they are too grand and remote, their grandeur and remoteness will be all they communicate; and children, in the classroom as elsewhere, thrive on familiarity, nearness, and affection, and on being able to do something themselves. What matters for the present is not that the children admire Blake and his achievement, but that each child be able to find a tyger of his own.

Of course they can learn more about poetry later, and they will do it better for having read poetry this way now. Even beginning this kind of study in high school, it is not too late to establish the necessary relation between what is in the poems and what is in the student's own mind and feelings and capacity to create for himself. There are of course, special problems with adolescent students—shyness, literariness of some who write, aggression and contempt of some who won't—but a teacher who knows students that age and can be enthusiastic and at the same time free and easy with them about poetry should be able to teach it very well.

There are some extensions and embellishments of this way of teaching that can be tried in elementary school—spending a few weeks on Blake, for example, with every student writing several poems in some way suggested by him and putting together a book of them with illustrations, like Blake's *Songs of Innocence and Experience;* or reading a number of poems which talk to nature in different ways; or reading the work of different poets who lived at the same time. The thing to aim for always, however, is the individual student responding to the individual poem in his own way.

The chapters that follow give details about ten classes on adult poems; how I explained the poems, how the children reacted to the poems, the poetry idea I gave them, and what the poems they wrote were like. This explanatory part of each chapter is followed by a selection of the children's poems. Not all of these are from PS 61. I corresponded with a few teachers elsewhere, whom I knew to be teaching writing, and asked them to try out Blake or Stevens or Shakespeare on their classes. So there are poems influenced by these poets from schools in New Orleans and North Dartmouth, Massachusetts. There are others written by ninth-grade students taught by an American Peace Corps worker at a missionary school in Swaziland, in Africa. I also taught a few classes in secondary schools, and there are poems here by tenth-grade students at the Lycée Français in New York, written in French and English in conjunction with the study of Rimbaud's poem "Voyelles." These poems from different schools show what some students found in the adult poems with the help of the discussion and the poetry idea, and what they were able to do with what they found. A teacher can get from them a rough idea of what to expect. Not that the results of any combinaton of teacher, children, and adult poetry are predictable—what the children write will vary according to all three. But a good and enthusiastic response to the adult poems does seem a common factor of all these works by children of different ages, in different schools, with different teachers, and even, in the case of the Swazi poems, from different cultures.

Some of the children's poems may be good to use in teaching the adult poems they were written with—to give students confidence by showing them what other children did, to stir up their feelings of emulation, to help them get ideas. Chip's line about Carmen might be just the thing to show some dreamy eleven-year-old his connection with Blake and with ideas of cosmic transformation and to get him started feeling, thinking, and writing.

The last part of this book is an anthology of other poems that might be good to teach to children, along with some detailed suggestions about how they can be taught.

Ten Lessons

Chapter One

WILLIAM BLAKE

The Tyger

Tyger! Tyger! burning bright
In the forests of the night,
What immortal hand or eye
Could frame thy fearful symmetry?

In what distant deeps or skies
Burnt the fire of thine eyes?
On what wings dare he aspire?
What the hand dare seize the fire?

And what shoulder, & what art,
Could twist the sinews of thy heart?
And when thy heart began to beat,
What dread hand? & what dread feet?

What the hammer? what the chain?
In what furnace was thy brain?
What the anvil? what dread grasp
Dare its deadly terrors clasp?

When the stars threw down their spears
And water'd heaven with their tears,
Did he smile his work to see?
Did he who made the Lamb make thee?

Tyger! Tyger! burning bright
In the forests of the night,
What immortal hand or eye
Dare frame thy fearful symmetry?

The Tyger

The idea of talking to an animal appeals to children a great deal. The whole air of mystery and magic about "The Tyger" is very interesting to them too. The main question the poet asks is a question they often think aout: How did something get the way it is? They ask this question about animals, about apples, about the sky and clouds, and about themselves. Blake has an excited idea of how the tiger got to be the way it is: that a Superpowered Being gathered materials from ocean, earth, and sky, and then pounded and twisted them all together until He had made a tiger. Blake stresses the amazingness and scariness of this Being: He has wings and can fly, can hold fire in his hand, and can control the terrible force of the tiger.

To help get the children to these fascinating aspects of the poem, past the difficulties of Blake's language and syntax, I stopped a number of times in discussing it to draw them into it by way of their own experiences. Had they ever seen a dog's or cat's eyes glowing in the dark? Did the eyes seem to be made of fire? What could be so strange about the tiger's heart? I asked the children to close their eyes, put their fingers in their ears, be very quiet, and listen. That strange thumping they heard was their heart. A tiger's heart might sound even stranger than that. The children seemed particularly stirred by this experience—I think it was new to them. Also new to them was the idea of symmetry, which I stopped to talk about. I made a diagram on the blackboard to show what symmetry meant, and then pointed out that they were symmetrical too. Excitedly touching their own knees, elbows, arms, and ears, the children had a feeling of amazement about symmetry close to the kind Blake seems to be expressing in the poem— an amazement likely to be felt less strongly by someone already familiar with symmetry as an abstract conception. At the start of the fifth stanza are two lines whose meaning I'm not sure of so I asked the children for their ideas. They had very good ones: Spears were the stars' sharp pointy shining, spears were lightning and tears were rain, spears and tears were the lightning and rain that came after the creation of the animals. They were delighted that I found their ideas good and that they had been able to join me in trying to figure out what part of the poem meant.

The poetry idea I gave the children was "Write a poem in which you are talking to a beautiful and mysterious creature and you can ask it anything you want—anything. You have the power to do this because you can speak its secret language." Children asked me if the creature could answer. I said yes. That would make the situation of the conversation more believable for them. I was also asked if a different creature could be questioned in every line, and I said yes to that too. Some children might be more inspired if they could rove over the whole realm of creatures instead of being obliged to stay with one. I told the children they needn't use rhyme, even though Blake's poem did. It was usual for poems to rhyme when "The Tyger" was written, but most poems written now don't rhyme. Blake wrote a lot of non-rhyming poems too. I suggested as a form for their poems a series of questions, like those Blake asks the tiger. If they wished, they could also repeat certain words the way Blake does.

The poems the children wrote were influenced not only by "The Tyger," but also by "The Lamb" and "The Sick Rose." "The Tyger" was the only poem I discussed, but the other two poems were also on the pages I passed out to them. It was a way to give my students a little more of Blake's work to read and respond to on their own, and some more inspiration for their poems. Many of them wrote about mild and relatively helpless creatures like the lamb rather than about frightening creatures like the tiger, and a few wrote about flowers. Whatever the kind of living thing, almost all the children's questions are about how it got some particular feature or quality —burning red wings, beautiful skin, long ears, small size, large size, the "power to slaughter your fellow animal." Sometimes these questions lead to concern for the creature's safety (as in the poems about insects by Billy, Lorraine, and Tracy); sometimes to a wish to have some of those qualities for oneself —Elizabeth would like to have the parrot's blue eyes, and

Nelida would like to have the blue eyes, the "pretty black hair," and the "nice shiny nose" of the horse. In many poems the questions are followed by answers, which attribute the creature's characteristics to a variety of historical, scientific, and cosmic factors. Sometimes the view of the creature is a fairly everyday view, and sometimes it is a strange and somewhat frightening one, like Valerie's vision of a snake, Damary's of a butterfly, Hipolito's of a giraffe. Several children used the situation to pay courtly compliments to girls (Chip to Carmen, Jeffrey to Veronica, Wilbert to Leda). A number of the poems were "jokes" (those by Diane, Markus, Richard, and Edgar.) The poems express a great variety of feeling and considerable intensity of feeling, as well as a great deal of playful creative invention and intellectual ingenuity. Being in the presence of a creature, with Blake's poems to put them in an excited mood about it, and with the freedom to say anything they wanted, was, for almost everyone in my classes from third to sixth grade, a really fine experience with poetry.

Some poems in this chapter are from the Newman School in New Orleans. Others are by ninth-grade students from Swaziland, whose teacher, Mary Bowler, was teaching them to write poetry, using my book *Wishes, Lies, and Dreams,* and to whom I suggested trying a lesson on Blake. The Swazi children, living near the jungle, are much closer to nature than my students are, and the situation of talking to a creature inspired them to write poems different from theirs in significant ways. My students used animals mainly to talk about their own secret feelings and imaginings. The Swazi students did that as well, to some extent, but the animals in their poems are far more substantial, more like real presences that have to be dealt with in life. The Swazi questions are often more practical—"Hawk, why do you steal my chickens?"; the observation more precise—"your tail so fluffy that even flies don't touch it"; the animal-human comparisons more immediate—"Your paws are as dangerous as the robbers at night." I was really delighted to see these poems, because they suggested that reading and writing poetry could be taught to children in a wide variety of educational and cultural situations. Though differing from my students' poems in details, the Swazi poems were like them in showing the excitement and inspiration their authors found in Blake, whose "Tyger," it was apparent, could stir children's talents and imaginations in Southeast Africa as well as between Avenue B and Avenue C.

THIRD AND FOURTH GRADES

The Sick Rose

"O rose, why are you sick? The little worm kills you
    now?"
"Yes, the little worm kills me now—this is the end of
    me!"
Up in the sky, down in the earth, "Why do you die in
    the light of earth?"
"I die now because the worm eats me."
Up in the sky, down in the earth, the worm is
    crawling in the ground.
Up in the sky, down in the earth, why do you die in
    the light of the earth.

Vivian Jenkins

Monkey

Oh, you must come from a hairy god.
Where do you get your funny voice?
Monkey, where did you learn to climb?
Monkey, how did you live to eat bananas?
Your feet must come from a chicken farm.

Michelle Woods

I would ask ponies
Is their nose too long? What heaven created your
    neigh?
Do you like sugar? Is the saddle too tight?
Where's your lost bridle?
Why did you bite it off?
Yes
No
In the south field.
I didn't like it.

Reade Bailey

Dog, where did you get that bark?
Dragon, where do you get that flame?
Kitten, where did you get that meow?
Rose, where did you get that red?
Bird, where did you get those wings?

Desiree Lynne Collier

Oh Rose, where did you get your color?
Dog so beautiful, how do you learn how to bark? Will
    you teach me?
Ant, the most precious, where did you get your body?
Beautiful butterfly, where did you get your wings?

Rose: there once was a red sea and I fell in.
Dog: my mother gave me lessons.
Ant: three rocks were stuck together, then lightning
    hit me.
Butterfly: one day a kid in Mrs. Fay's class drew a
    butterfly, then it got loose and it was raining,
    then it was alive the next day.

Arlene Wong

Glub blub, little squid. Glub blub, why blub do
you glub have blub Glubblub blub such glub
inky blub stuff blubbb? I use it for a protective
shield against my enemies blubbb. Why blub
blub blub do you have such glub funny blubb
eyes blub? The better to see you with. Why blub
do glub you blub glub have such blub funny blub
tentacles? The blub better to grab you blub with.
Arragh! Blub blug blug blub glug blub.

Markus Niebanck

I asked a tiger where did Leda get her pretty body,
    especially at the lips and legs and face.
She must get it from Mrs. Fay and her sisters and her
    brother got it from the Funny Farm.
Leda acts strange sometimes, but she is a swinging
    chick.
She might not think so, but I do.
        Wilbert
        Ha ha ha ha

Wilbert Miller

Danny dragon, where did you get your flame?
Is it from Veronica when she kissed you? You got so
    happy.

Jeffrey Hatch

Dog

Dog, where did you get your bark?
Dog, where did you come from?
Dog, why are you here?
Your shiny fur shines in the night.
How come you don't talk?
I wish you were around, so you could answer me,
So I wouldn't be all alone.

Leda Mesen

Rabbit, how come you twitch your nose?
Rabbit, how can you run so fast?
And why are you so fiery and why do you run away
    from people?
Why do you eat grass and carrots?
Why don't you eat bugs?
Why do you hibernate?

Lynn Bonner

Little duck, little duck, how did you get those iron
    legs?
How did you get those steel eyes?
How did you get 43 ears?
How does your head glow in the light?
What god made you?

Edgar Guadeloupe

Horse, how come you are so pretty, so big? I
only wish you could talk back. I wish you were
all mine. I would take very much care of you. I
wish I was like you, but a person—nice blue eyes,
nice shiny nose, such pretty black hair. Please
try not to be sold.

Nelida Quinones

I asked my friend, is it an animal? Is it nice, and
   beautiful? Is it a parrot?
It has blue eyes and I told the parrot where did she
   get her eyes, so I could find some for me.

Elizabeth Cortez

Mice, mice, mice, why do you look nice? Squeak
   squeak!
Mice, mice, mice, mice, squeak, squeak, squeak.
Why are your eyes red? Squeak! Do you sleep in a
   bed?
Where did you get ruby eyes?
   Squeak-squeak-squeak-squeak-
Squeak squeak mouse mouse mouseee
Eeeeeeeeeeeeeeeeeeeeeeeeeeeeeeeeeeeeeeeeee
SQUEAK MOUSE

Ricky Marcilla

Dinosaur, what is your name?
My name is Dirty Dinosaur.
Why are you called that?
Because I eat the people in bed.
Butterfly what is your name?

Ronald Kelly

Butterfly, how did you get your wings and where did
    you get your antenna with the round balls and
    the wings that swings.
And you are very funny, like a baby moth.
And your eyes are like fire and you are little and you
    want to learn how to whistle.
In the night the stars are bright and your eyes glow
    in the night.
Look at your eyes that look like the skies.
How about in the day you stay.
And what's your name when you play games?

Joseph Cruz

Bird

I was talking in a jungle.
Oh Bird, where did you get your color, blue, pink, and
    yellow.
The bird said, "I painted myself."
I asked the bird, how could you fly? The bird said,
    "By you carrying me."
What is your name? "My name is Dirty Dinosaur
    Bird vampire,"

Diane Maza

I Talked to an Animal

Oh, my very dear horse,
Do you like to ride me?
I love your so very soft mane.
I hope to go trotting down a sugarcane lane.
Who is your friend?
I like to talk to you. Now you talk to me.

And he talked to me.

Hello, I'm Harry, the Horse.
What is your name?
I can imagine it is a pretty name because you've got
    silky hair, a pretty little freckled face and you're
    just the right size.
That's the kind of a person I like.

Ellen Schornstein

Dear Mrs. Manatee,
I know you are a sea cow
A large sea mammal with flippers and a flat oval tail.
Oh, how many babies do you have?

Nanette Colomb

Tiger Dog

Oh, Tiger Dog, why do you eat my clothes?
Oh, why do you jump on the flowers in my garden?
Oh, why do you mark up my furniture?
Why are you such an awful Tiger Dog?

I eat your clothes because they taste good.
I jump on your flowers because it makes me bounce.
I mark up your furniture so it will have a design.
I am a bad dog for the fun of being bad.

Wendy Hyman

Once I went to my basement
I saw a mouse walk by
I asked the mouse "Why do you creep?"
He answered "Because my back hurts"
"Why don't you do anything about it?"
He said "If I did I'd stand up straight"
Just then a snail walked by.
I said "Why don't you get out of your shell?"
He said "People would mistake me as a worm and I
    hate worms"
I felt something touch me
I looked up and it was a spider
I said "Why don't you live on the floor or in a crack
    like other animals?"
He said "They disturb me too much"
I'll never forget my day in the basement.

Karen Overby

Tigers

Mr. Tiger, why do you have stripes?
Because it makes me fierce.
Mr. Tiger, why do you have black and orange stripes?
Because the sun had black and orange stripes.
Dr. Tiger, why are you a doctor?
Because I like to fix the other animal's bones that I
    break.
Mr. Tiger, why do you have bloodshot eyes?
Because I stay up all night fighting the animals that
    try to kill my wife.

Robert Soboloff

One day I went walking in the forest
I became lost
Then I saw a crocodile
I said, "Sir, crocodile, why are you green?"
And he said, "Miss, why are you brown?"
And I said, "Because the sun thought I was some
    bread and he baked me."
Then the crocodile said, "Well, the swamp thought I
    was a brown plant, so he turned me green."

Judy Wallen

FIFTH GRADE

Birds

Mr. Robin, how did you ever get those beautiful red,
    yellow, blue feathers?
Long ago Indians gave me the feathers from their
    heads.

Dear Mr. Bluejay, where did you get those beautiful
    eyes of yours?
They came from the sky of yours.

Bluebird, why were you named Bluebird? Please
    answer.
I got the name from an ancient god over ten
    thousand years ago.

Mr. Tiger, where did you get your beautiful skin?
I guess I got it from blowing wind.

Rosa Rosario

Oh snake, how come you are so tall? Where did you
    get those beautiful colors?
How come I can see you from a mile away? Did the
    same god that made you make humans?
Where did you get your tongue and your fireful eyes?
    How can you spin so fast?

Valerie Goodall

Polar Bear

Bear, what color are you? Brown, white, and black.
Do you have friends? Yes, I have ants, bears, and
    myself.
Do you have a mountain cave? Yes, I have a cave
    with bats.
Do you have friends like little girls? Yes, lots of them.
Bear, what do you eat? I eat ducks and honey and I
    eat you.
Bear, you jump up and down—why? Because I am a
    jumping bean.

Rebecca Crespo

Rabbit, where did you get your long pair of ears?
Where did you get your cute little eyes?
Don't you get tired of carrots?
Where did you get your lovely coat of fur?
Why do you always eat carrots?
Why can't you eat other foods?
Are your teeth like human's teeth?
Do you like Mr. Koch if you are a human being?
Do you take a bath every day and do you like baths?
Is it fun to be a rabbit?

Fung Ping Lui

A Tiger

Mr. Tiger, where did you get those orange and black
    stripes?
Mr. Tiger, where did you get those sharp, dark,
    vicious claws?
Mr. Tiger, where did you get those ferocious white
    teeth?
Mr. Tiger, where did you get that snake-like tail?
Mr. Tiger, where did you get those fire-like eyes?
Mr. Tiger, where did you get that roar?
Mr. Tiger, where do you come from?

Little boy, I got my stripes from the animal God.
Little boy, I got my claws from the animal God.
Little boy, I got my teeth from the animal God.
Little boy, I got my tail from the animal God.
Little boy, I got my eyes from the animal God.
Little boy, I got my roar from the animal God and I
    come from heaven.

Andrew Norden

I asked a butterfly how did it get here and where did
    it come from.
I looked at his eyes with flame coming out of his
    eyes, and his body like something I've never seen
    in my whole life, its feet marked the whole place.
I ran away. It was behind me the whole time, I fell,
    and that was the last time I saw the butterfly.

Damary Hernandez

Little daisies yellow and white, who made thee all
through the night. Thee are so pretty, thee are so
gay, in the spring a month so gay daisies are born
to live a day.
Daisies, Daisies, yellow and white I love you with all
my might.
Daisies, Daisies, talk—tell me the answer, oh please,
oh please.

Antoinette Anderson

Stingbee, Stingbee, why did you bother everybody?
Because no one ever lets me enjoy myself.
Stingbee, Stingbee, why did you die after you stung
me? Because that's the way they made me.
Stingbee, Stingbee, who made you? I wish I knew, but
now I must leave forever.

Richard Rivera

The Strange Rabbit

Rabbit, where did you get those long long ears?
They grew like stalks upon my head.
Rabbit, rabbit, how come you hop up and down?
It's because I take ups and downs and I can't stop.

Rabbit, rabbit, why do you live in the ground?
It's because I make more drugs there.
Rabbit, rabbit, why do you love carrots?
It's because they're good for my eyes and my eyes
    don't water when I take drugs.
Rabbit, rabbit, when will you die?
As soon as I take an overdose.

Myrna Diaz

Giraffes, how did they make Carmen? Well, you see,
    Carmen ate the prettiest rose in the world and
    then just then the great change of heaven
    occurred and she became the prettiest girl in the
    world and because I love her.
Lions, why does your mane flame like fire of the
    devil? Because I have the speed of the wind and
    the strength of the earth at my command.
Oh Kiwi, why have you no wings? Because I have
    been born with the despair to walk the earth
    without the power of flight and am damned to do
    so.
Oh bird of flight, why have you been granted the
    power to fly? Because I was meant to sit upon the
    branch and to be with the wind.
Oh crocodile, why were you granted the power to
    slaughter your fellow animal? I do not answer.

Chip Wareing

SIXTH GRADE

Giraffe! Giraffe!
What kicky, sticky legs you've got.
What a long neck you've got. It looks like a stick of
    fire.
You have dots blue, yellow, and orange. You look like
    you are burning.
Giraffe! Giraffe!
What kicky sticky legs you've got.

Hipolito Rivera

Oh butterfly oh butterfly
Where did you get your burning red wings?
I got my burning red wings from the heaven above.
Oh butterfly oh butterfly, what do you do at night?
I visit all the planets.
Oh butterfly oh butterfly, what planets do you visit?
I visit the burning sun, the heart of the moon.
Oh butterfly oh butterfly, why are you so small?
I am small because one day I had a terrible fight
    with the burning sun and the heart of the moon
    and the both of them squished me like a
    squashed banana but I escaped and only a little
    of me was left.

Lisa Smalley

Look at yourself, fly, you have such a short life.
Too bad because I would like to make friends with
    you but when you die I would be sad.
I see your friends riding on your back and wish I
    could shrink and ride with you.
You look pale, do you thing anything's wrong?
I think I am dying, Billy, good-bye.

Billy Constant

The Ant

Oh little ant that lives in a hole
How do you feel today?
The roses are in bloom and the purple sunlight is
    shining.
How do you feel when dirt bombs are thrown?
When they explode it probably looks like fireworks in
    the night.
When it rains how do you sail through the rough
    waters of the world?
When the stars are quiet and the purple moon is still,
    how do you feel?
When the stars fall to the earth and the purple moon
    comes out no more
You will live with joy away from the harsh earth.

Andrew Vecchione

The Elephant

Elephant oh elephant
Why are you so fat?
How much can one eat to get so fat?
Where did you get your trunk?
Elephant oh elephant
Where did you get your teeth? Who has all that ivory
    to give to you?
Elephant oh elephant who made you?

Tommy Kennedy

The Poor Wimpoorwill

The poor wimpoorwill who lies up in the tree
Why do you cry?

Poor wimpoorwill
It is now dawn
Do not cry your sad song.

Poor wimpoorwill
Why are your colors so drab?
Is that why you cry?
Poor wimpoorwill
Fly away
For it is now dusk.

Tracy Lahab

The Little Bug

Why are you so small, little bug?
You will get trampled on, little bug.
Why do you climb in the ground so dirty, little bug?
You will get dirty, little bug.
Do you like cream cheese, little bug?
I will give you some.
Come into my house, little bug.
We will feast on cream cheese and bees!

Tracy Lahab

The Firefly

Oh firefly what makes you turn on?
It looks as though someone puts a bulb in you.
But who puts the bulb on? What happens when your
    bulb blows out?
Do the butterflies replace your bulb?
Or does the dark of night replace it?
I wish I could understand what you're trying to say
    when you flicker your lights.

Marion Mackles

Lamb

Oh lamb, who puts on your woolly hair
Soft as snow, white as the heavens, warm as the sun?
Lamb, who puts it on?
Oh person, I am as soft as snow from kindness.
I'm as white as the heavens for that's where I come
    from.
I'm as warm as the sun from my love.
Kind person, I have all this for being what I am, a
    lamb.

Marion Mackles

The Pansy

Dear little velvet pansy.
Tell me how you pull yourself out of the ground
And feed yourself without moving.
Tell me what you think of the poppy flower,
Who visits with you in the bed.
Do you mind being picked and used
To refresh a house and make it pretty?
Or is that part of your daily, lifely chore
As a little velvet pansy?

Melanie Myers

Oh Ants, Oh Ants

Oh ants, oh ants, do you wear pants?
Oh ants, oh ants, where do you sleep?
Oh ants, oh ants, how many of you get killed a day?
Oh ants, oh ants, how do you think, with such a little
    head?
Oh ants, oh ants, how do you see with such little
    eyes?
Oh ants, oh ants!!

Oh You, Oh You
Oh you, oh you, I do not wear pants.
Oh you, oh you, I sleep in the street.
Oh you, oh you, I can't remember how many of us get
    killed a day.
Oh you, oh you, I just think no matter what size my
    head is.
Oh you, oh you, I see with little eyes because I'm
    used to seeing with little eyes.
Oh you, oh you!!

                                        Lorraine Fedison

O lion of the jungle, who made your mane?
Who made the fire down your neck?
What is your source of power?
You are king of the jungle.
O lion who rules an empire,
What made you so fast and strong?

Your power is made of a third of the sun.
You shall always rule the jungle.
You who fight the animals of the jungle,
Have any conquered you?
O lion of the jungle, the sun must have made you,
For you are king of all beasts.

Charles Waite

Oh Daffodil, I hope you never die but last forever.
Oh Daffodil, live till the sun turns red and the moon
    turns black.

Jeannie Turner

NINTH GRADE (SWAZILAND)

The Lion

Oh, Majesty Lion, saluted I.
Who made you to be the king of animals?
Who made your eyes as fearful as the burning fires of
    the Usuthu forests?
Even your paws are as dangerous as the robbers at
    night.
Your voice is so big as thunderstorms in the hot
    summer seasons.
Who made your tail so fluffy that even flies don't
    touch it?

Who made you so fearful that even the creatures of
the world are afraid of you?

The Hawk

Hawk, why do you eat my chickens?
My chickens are decreasing because of you.
Why don't you come and ask for some . . . don't steal
my chickens.
Where were you when the chickens became tame
birds?
I want to know who taught you this system of coming
quickly when you steal.
Hawk, hawk, why are you a foe to my chickens?
Is it because you are a wild bird?
Where do you live when it is cold?
How are your feathers when it is raining . . . are they
not folded together.
So be patient Hawk, to my chickens.
Try to fly further up to the heaven and consult God.
Ask him to give you a better system of feeding yours.

The Elephant

Oh! Mr. Elephant, how big and tough animal you are.
Are you the king of all the animals in the world?
What are those big and tough feet for?
Even your appearance is like a mountain 1700 feet
high.

"Oh, my feet and body are for protection against my
enemies."

Do you know Mr. Ant, your tiny small enemy?
The one who cannot even see the sky that you can
   touch.
He can only feel the sun's heat on the surface of the
   earth.

"I don't want to even see him because he is my
   dangerous enemy."

Who gave you all these strong and tough feet and big
   ears?

"The One who created me. He said that I will be the
   king of the animals except for the Ant who will
   also be king."

The Ant

Little ant, what makes you to be so happy and busy?
Why don't you sit and rest or dance about enjoying
   such a sunny weather?
Why don't you look to the big foot coming to destroy
   your body?
Oh! Little creature. Oh! Busy all the time.
Who was the Creator who thought of such a small
   creature like you?
Is it the same Creator who made such a big fearful
   lion?

The Mole

Oh, mole. You wonderful animals.
What makes you stay in the ground?
Why do you eat the soil?
Do you make it into a nice soup?
Why do you have no eyes?
But, are there ways and streets inside the ground?
Do you have friends there?
What are their names?
Because all animals live on the ground eating grass
     and other things growing in the ground, what
     kind of vitamins do you get.
What makes you to have no tail like the rock rabbit?
We are told that the rock rabbit is lazy, are you lazy?
No, you always dig soil and place it on the surface of
     the earth.
You are an active animal, not lazy.

The Cow

Cow! Cow! Why do you walk with four legs?
Why do you fight your enemies with horns instead of
     a gun?
Why do you drag heavy things with your sledge?
Why do you eat grass instead of porridge?
Why do you have a tail?
Your maker must be a wonderful person to put all
     those parts on you.

You can help the people by dragging their heavy
   things.
Even so, I find that I really can't talk to you.

The Cat

What a beautiful creature on earth.
Who gave you such lovely hair?
Your hair seems to be rare,
But your eyes look a bit dangerous.
I think the one who made the lion, is the one who
   made thee.

"But Sir, you said I am a lovely creature.
Why does the dog hate me?
There is no one who praises me about my hair."

I think the dog hates you because you used to drink
   its milk,
And he likes meat too as thee.

"That is true, Sir, but we can't say anything because
   the
One who made us made us to eat the same food.
If your neighbor has want of the same thing, do you
   simply hate him?"

If you were born full of jealousy,
You will also die full of it.
Poor cat, mighty and lovely creature.

The Elephant

Elephant, elephant, big and fat.
Are you a young, strong, healthy elephant?
Have you ever fought with a lion?
Why did God make you so big, and
Why did God make this long tusk?
Where did God start you and end you?
Why did God make you so big and fat and ugly?
Why are you not the king of animals?
You are so big that even a lion, the king of animals,
    would be frightened of you.
Elephant, Elephant, funny, running, speeding . . .
Getting into the forest, chasing some hares for
    breakfast.

The Snake

Snake, snake, hiding in the thick bush forest.
Sometimes surrounding the trunk of a tree like rope
    or string.
What kind of head do you have?
Because I see only a funny thing on your front end.
What kind of teeth do you have . . . you can't laugh
    and you can't sing.
What kind of movement do you have?
Because I see no feet, no claws, no legs.

When you are moving you seem to be attached to the
 ground.
Snake, snake what kind of eyes do you have?
They look like dead things.

The Hare

You are a wonderful creature.
Your mind is full of tricks,
With your eyes so big
With your feet so short and thin.

Who taught you not to shut your eyes when asleep?
Who taught you to sleep at noon not at night?
Who taught you those many tricks you have?
Where do you get the speed you have?

Maybe you share the speed with lightning.
Maybe the ghost told you to enjoy the night with him.
Maybe the angel from heaven taught you all the
 tricks.
Your eyes are so big that they can't even close.

Your hair looks like shining gold.
As you run your tail seems to be saying goodbye.
Your ears seem to be signaling for danger.
And your whole body is like a rolling stone.

Why does the dog chase you?
Why does the human being kill you?
Maybe it's because a person hates your friend, the
 ghost.
Maybe it's because of your shining, gold-like body.

The Goat

What a strange creature you are.
Who made your shining hairs?
Who decided to give you a beard?
When it is cold do you feel like shivering?
I don't think so, because your coat is so wonderful
    with shining hairs on it.
Why did you choose to eat grass?
Isn't it bad to be a grass eater?
But the sound you make is so sweet that when the
    clouds hear it they start to move fast and change
    their colors in order to show their enjoyment to
    you.
Why did you choose such feet for walking?
Don't they wear down quickly . . . they look like
    leather.
Why do dogs hate you?
But I think that one day you will all make peace and
    become friendly again.

Chapter Two

ROBERT HERRICK

The Argument of His Book

I sing of brooks, of blossoms, birds, and bowers,
Of April, May, of June, and July flowers.
I sing of Maypoles, hock carts, wassails, wakes,
Of bridegrooms, brides, and of their bridal cakes.
I write of youth, of love, and have access
By these to sing of cleanly wantonness.
I sing of dews, of rains, and, piece by piece,
Of balm, of oil, of spice, and ambergris.
I sing of times trans-shifting, and I write
How roses first came red and lilies white.
I write of groves, of twilights, and I sing
The court of Mab and of the fairy king.
I write of hell; I sing (and ever shall)
Of heaven, and hope to have it after all.

The Argument of His Book

A poem which lists things is easy for children to imitate, and this one is good for reminding children of poems they've already written, and for making them think about what new kinds of poems they'd like to write. In the course of my teaching I often reminded my students of the kinds of poems they had written before. I wanted them to remember, so they could use all those themes and ways of saying things in their new poems. Children like to remember their poems—it's somewhat like thinking of beautiful places one has been, or of brave things one has done, or of funny or important or beautiful things one has said. The excitement of it puts them in a good mood for writing something new.

The poetry idea was, "Write a poem about all the things you've written poems about, or that you would like to write poems about. If you like, you can start every line with 'I write about' or 'I would like to write about.' " I added other remarks to help them get started. "You can imagine that your poem, like Herrick's, will be on the first page of a book of your poems. You can include all kinds of things you've really written about." I would remind them: wishes, comparisons, colors, dreams, talking to animals. I said, "You can be more specific than that, too. Instead of just saying you write about wishes, you can say what the wish is—'I write about wishing for a blue coat'; or what you compared to what, or what animal you talked to—'I write about talking to a rabbit and asking him his name.' " If they wrote about what they would like to put into their poems, I urged them to really think of the most secret, crazy things, anything they wanted. I wanted them to be in a dreamy, excited mood, thinking about their creations in the past and their desires for the future.

In going through Herrick's poem, I pointed out to the children all the different subjects he says he writes about: nature, flowers, country customs like Maypole dances, weddings, love, perfumes, times changing, how things got to be the way they are; also fairyland, hell, and heaven. I also pointed out that Herrick often wrote poems about seemingly small and unimportant things, such as "bridal cakes."

In their poems for this class, the children, like Herrick, wrote about nature—

My poems are about the forest.
The wind blowing in your face and you go to pick
    up daisies—

about seemingly small and unimportant things—

Of pink ice and blue ice and red ice,
And of people as big as my thumb—

and about sex and love—

I like to write poems about poems, I like poems.
Some girls are like poems—

or, inspired by the idea that they could write about anything whatsoever, about "crazy things"—a pineapple dog, a radio strawberry, flowers kissing New York.

I think the thing in Herrick's poem that made the children feel freest about their own poems was his saying he sang of little things, of love and of hell, which gave them permission, the third and fourth graders particularly, to be somewhat "silly," romantic, and wicked.

If the children have written a number of poems, it may help inspire them to have some of their poems quickly read over in class before they write. These will give them ideas, but of course they shouldn't feel bound to what they or other children have written. Their own poem lists can be perfectly fanciful and free.

Hesperides, the name of the book for which Herrick wrote "The Argument" suggests either golden apples (from the garden of Hesperides) or little stars (daughters of the evening star, named Hesperus). It might be worthwhile to suggest to the children that Herrick thought of his poems as things that were small, shining, and beautiful and suggest that they might think of their poems in this way too.

If the children are interested in Herrick, the study of his

work could be continued with some poems on themes he mentions in "The Argument." The children might like some on how flowers got their colors ("How Marigolds Came Yellow," "How Violets Came Blew"). Or, the teacher might simply read some of Herrick's shorter poems along with the children's poems.

THIRD AND FOURTH GRADES

I like to write about wishes, lies, and dreams,
Of pink ice and blue ice and red ice,
And of people as big as my thumb.
Also of red, yellow, blue, purple licorice.
I would like to write about pink bananas.
And of color TVs.
I would like to write about Arlene.

Lynn Bonner

I'd like to write about a pineapple dog
I'd like to write about the drunk people in the street.
I'd like to write about horror movies.
I'd like to write about Wilbert bothering Nina and
     Leda.
I'd like to write a life story about Wilbert.

Mario Angelo Morales

Poem

I like to write poems about poems. I like poems.
Some girls are like poems.

Eric Felisbret

My poem is about a banana who walked away from
    the store with his friend the apple
The banana was green and the apple was yellow
    pink but I saw the apple and banana walking and
    my head fell off
I put it back on again
I went walking home with my left hand in my right
    hand
When I got home I didn't know what was with me I
    fell on the floor and went crazy.

Edgar Guadeloupe

I'd like to write about:
Pineapples were dancing girls,
Strawberries were radios,
I was I was a bathtub
You were the sea
Then you went in me.

Jeff Hatch

I use a dancing pen in my desk.
And in the rain forest I saw Michelle, Nelida, and
    Eric looking like monkeys swinging on vines with
    bananas on their heads.
I remember that I saw Nelida run for Eric and Edgar
Then Eric and Edgar ran and got or caught Nelida.
I remember I saw Chris and Veronica in a swimming
    pool.

Diana Maza

I wrote about a skinny Santa Claus.
I write about when I pull Chris's hair.
I like to write about when Eric was bent down for the
    whole afternoon.

Author unknown

I Would Like to Write About. . . .

I would like to write about somebody swimming in
    my stomach.
I would like to write about me in Candyland eating
    licorice and lollipop.
It would be fun if I was in wishing land
Well that's all I like to write about.

Arlene Wong

Elizabeth, Leda, Arlene, Nina
Roses are red

Violets are blue
Vinegar is sweet
And I like all of these girls in my way
         la la la
         kiss kiss
         wow

                Wilbert Miller

What I Like to Write About

What I like to write about is not very funny to me,
    but you might like it. Once I saw a strawberry, it
    had a lot of freckles.
And then I saw an orange, with red hair,
And my brother's tennis shoes look like rags, because
    the cats chew them up.

                Nina Thomason

I write about hairy machines.
And purple monkeys
I have guts.
And Santa Claus in his underpants.
And his long underwear.
It must cost a lot of bread.
And monkeys that fly.

                Reade Bailey

My Poem is About?

I made a note that I saw Elizabeth looking at
     pineapple TV.
And I sing of comics
And Stuart Little marrying a girl
And tropical rain forest got Marcus on leg
Dragons marry Asia
And flowers kissed New York
I will finish later
Here's a picture of flowers kissing New York.

Author unknown

I wish that Arlene and I were walking on a rope
     bridge at night and under us was a big hole with
     soft foam rubber and feathers under us and the
     bridge collapsed.
I wish that Nina fell through a bear trap 10,000 feet
     down and no way out and I caught her.
I wish Leda walked down a blind alley and fell
     through the floor into a big dungeon of the blue
     monster and fell in my cell.

Markus Niebanck

FIFTH GRADE

My poems are about the forest.
The wind blowing in your face and you go to pick up
    daisies
The smell of flowers.
Everyone taking a walk.
Or just taking the day off and just disappear for the
    day and go to the forest.
Or a picnic in the forest.

Carmen Berrios

I would like to write a poem about the things people
    think.
I would like to write a poem about Antoinette's hair.
I would like to write a poem about China.
I would like to write a poem about Antoinette and
    Myrna.
I would like to write about Taiwan.
I would like to write about the moon.
I would like to write about my class.

Richard Rivera

I would like to write about flowers, animals, and rain.
I used to write love poems, but now I write about
    noise and color and about a lot of funny things.

I would like to write about murder and super-hero or
   even the Shadow.

Valerie Goodall

I really would like to write about a kitten that has
   yellow hair.
I really would like to write about a purple rabbit
   with light blue eyes.
I really would like to write about a winter day.

Lynne Reiff

I would like to write about Brotherhood
I would like to write about the agony of love
I would like to write about the country
I would like to write about dresses

Maria Gutierrez

I would like to write about sex
I would like to write about love
I would like to write about kissing
I would like to write about dancing and everything
   else.

Benny Vincifora

I like to write about people but I have to write about
    animals.
I did like to write about house condition, but I have
    to write about the living.
I did like to write about school's condition, but I have
    to write about my classroom.
I did like to write poems, but I have to write about
    history.
I did like to write about Miss Pitts, but I have to write
    about Mr. Bowman.

Fung Ping Lui

I would like to write about things that aren't real.
I would like to write about flowers that could talk.

Melissa Blitz

I would like to write about Steven and bad things.

Joseph Scifo

I used to dream I was an ant, people stepping on me
    and grieving.
I used to dream I was a fruit, people biting me and
    eating me up.
I used to dream I was a cat, dogs chasing and teasing
    me.
I used to dream I was everything that I don't like at
    all.

Janet Vega

I once wrote a poem about an apple dress I once had
and how it didn't fit me.
I would like to write a poem about my friend
Antoinette who makes me laugh and tells me
stupid things.
I would like to write about a boy who acts funny and
likes a girl and you really can't tell the
difference.

Myrna Diaz

Chapter Three

JOHN DONNE

A Valediction: Forbidding Mourning

As virtuous men pass mildly away,
  And whisper to their souls to go,
Whilst some of their sad friends do say,
  "The breath goes now," and some say, "No,"

So let us melt, and make no noise,
  No tear-floods, nor sigh-tempests move;
'Twere profanation of our joys
  To tell the laity our love.

Moving of the earth brings harms and fears,
  Men reckon what it did and meant;
But trepidation of the spheres,
  Though greater far, is innocent.

Dull sublunary lovers' love
  (Whose soul is sense) cannot admit
Absence, because it doth remove
  Those things which elemented it.

But we, by a love so much refined
  That our selves know not what it is,
Inter-assured of the mind,
  Care less, eyes, lips, and hands to miss.

Our two souls therefore, which are one,
  Though I must go, endure not yet
A breach, but an expansion.
  Like gold to airy thinness beat.

If they be two, they are two so
  As stiff twin compasses are two:
Thy soul, the fixed foot, makes no show
  To move, but doth, if the other do;

And though it in the center sit,
  Yet when the other far doth roam,
It leans, and hearkens after it,
  And grows erect, as that comes home.

Such wilt thou be to me, who must,
  Like the other foot, obliquely run;
Thy firmness makes my circle just,
  And makes me end where I begun.

A Valediction: Forbidding Mourning

The appeal of this poem for children is that it offers them new things to write about (science and math), and shows them how they can use these things to talk about tender and passionate feelings in an indirect way, without being embarrassed—that is, talk about them by means of mechanical, mathematical, and scientific analogies. Doing this has a particular appeal for boys, who are often more embarrassed about their tender feelings than girls are. Donne's poem shows that if you know how compasses work, you can write about girls, about loving them. I don't think it had occurred to my students before that knowing about rockets, math, or about how an engine worked, would help them write love poetry or, for that matter, any kind of poetry. They were excited at finding it out.

The poetry idea was, "Write a poem in which you compare deep and serious feelings to things in science and math. If you like, put one of these comparisons in every line. Or you can devote the whole poem to one or two comparisons."

To show the children how such comparisons worked I went through the poem and explained many of the comparisons there. I brought a big compass to school and went through the comparison in the last three stanzas in detail, making sure everybody understood it. After that I made some comparisons of my own, and encouraged a lot of examples from the class. Each new scientific, mathematical, or mechanical thing that was mentioned brought smiles to faces and, apparently, inspirations to brains, since their poems turned out to be very good. I said, What feeling do you have that is like magnetism, for example? Hands went up. Obviously, the way I feel about somebody is like magnetism. Electricity? More hands. It was an exciting moment—all these things my students knew about but didn't think mattered, as far as emotions went, now suddenly really did, and they were having new thoughts about them. Turning on a light-switch, a bulb burning out, an electric eye, all these, considered as things that happened in human feelings and relationships, had a certain new magic quality. When there was sufficient excitement about all this in the classroom, I had the children write.

Most of their poems are about love. Love is compared to two waves dashing together, two lines which never diverge, the force of gravity, two planets in eclipse, thunder and lightning, pencil and paper, and a computer. Lovers are compared to rockets going to a planet, rockets free of gravitational pull, two bombs, two sticks, two bowling pins, two stars, and two light-bulbs. Some of the poems, like Billy Constant's, are very Donne-like in their ingenious working out of a single conception; others have individual images which, like Donne's, are both peculiar and psychologically true, like Miklos Lengyel's comparison of love to "gravity pulling a divorced couple together because when we separate we are pulled together again." The poems are full of verve. The children wrote them quickly and energetically. Some wrote two poems, and one student, Andrew Vecchione, wrote three, which all deal with the same theme (separation) and which show a steady improvement in both imaginativeness and accuracy (fine Donne-like qualities)—the first two about scissors, the third about rocketry. There were other good responses which took off from Donne but ended up being less like him. Some poems seemed influenced by the Blake class a few weeks before—the universe of "The Tyger" seems present in Rafael's cosmic lightning and beautiful darkness of space, for example, and there is a Blakean strangeness in Jeannie's comparison of a heartbeat to thunder. In a few cases the farfetched quality of Donne's imagery inspired a child to wild flights more characteristic of surrealism than of Donne's one-to-one equating— Miklos's last line, for example, about love and Venus's shadow; or Mayra's fantasy of two strings untying themselves in outer space.

I taught "A Valediction: Forbidding Mourning" only to sixth graders, but I think fourth- and fifth-grade students would like it too. Children in all grades love comparisons which bring things together in an unexpected way. One might want to teach other poems using metaphysical conceits too. Any one a teacher feels particularly drawn to will probably make for a good class. Marvell's "Definition of Love" is splendidly "meta-physical" and might be good to teach despite its difficulty. Children might also enjoy the extravagant metaphysical-style compliments in Carew's "A Song": Ask me no more. . . .

SIXTH GRADE

Hatred is like a pen drawing two lines far apart, and
    when they get to know each other, the pen
    connects them.
Fear is like the lines never connecting.
Love is like they were never apart.
Like is when they are a fourth of an inch apart.

                Billy Constant

Two lovers together are like two computers writing "I
    love you."
Two lovers are like two flowers growing together—
    this love is like two flowers when it is blooming
    from a seed.
Two lovers are like two sticks rubbing together and
    all of a sudden they make a fire and explode into
    love.
Two lovers are like two bombs when they explode.

                Ileana Mesen

Love is like the two ends of a rope when you tie them
    together.
Love is the blink of lightning when you see her for
    the first time.
Love is the sound of thunder, but really is the sound
    of her heartbeat.
Love is the sound of thunder, but really is the call of
    night.

Jeannie Turner

Fear

Fear is total darkness
Fear is like a fuse going out
Fear is like a doll,
It has eyes but it can't see through them
Fear is a bolt of lightning
Fear is a star that you can't see
Fear is frightening

Marion Mackles

Life is like a rubber tire
It rolls on and on
When the tire gets a flat life is gone
Envy is like a fire that can never be put out.
Fear is a bulb that blew out.
Love is a computer with all different flickering lights.
Death is like a rock,
Cold and all alone.

Marion Mackles

Our Feeling

Our love is like two waves dashing together
No one can separate us, not even the shore
My hatred for your ex-boyfriend is like the way oil
    and vinegar repel

Stephen Sebbane

Feelings

Once I had a feeling I was so short,
I felt like a short socket.
Once I had a feeling because I had a fight,
I felt like a burning rope.
Once I had a feeling about these flowers that loved
    each other,
So they went and kissed and they felt like a ball of
    fire.

Lorraine Fedison

Love is like a scissors. When they cut they are
    together—when they part they get divorced.
A dog and a cat are like clothes pin and a pen.
June and July are like the hot summer sun faded in
    the purple and red sky.

December and January are like snow on a dark and
    silent night.
War and peace are like an ant and a tiger.
A bad day and a sunny day are like a cemetery and a
    new animal.

Andrew Vecchione

Love is a Scissor

Love is like a scissor
When it's together it's happy
When it's apart it's sad
When it's rusty it has a sore throat.

Andrew Vecchione

A space capsule is like a man with two wives.
One part falls off because she finds out about the
    other wife.
The second part falls off when they get divorced and
    the third falls off when the man dies, and the
    lunar module floats to heaven like his soul.

Andrew Vecchione

Love

Love is like a pencil and paper
All pencils love all paper and vice-versa
When the pencil point hits the paper they kiss and
    send messages up to our brain and we write code
    letters that only pencils and paper can
    understand.

Tommy Kennedy

Two people in love are like cement glued onto their
    lips.
Two people in love are like two lips giving electricity.
Two people in love are like two knots tied together.
Two people in love is like doing faces at each other.
Two people in love is like mouth to mouth
    communication.

                         Author unknown

    Love is like two galaxies at war with another
galaxy, having war with fireballs and cosmic
lightning, striking at each other. Then peace
comes between them. The beautiful darkness of
space is once again peaceful and the stars
gleaming with radiance of beauty. We all can
learn from some planets that war isn't everything, 'cause no bolt of lightning is going to kill
you—you may not have any money, but you have
love.

                         Rafael Camacho

The love between my mice and me is like the love
    between a spaceman and his space capsule
The hatred between cats and dogs is like the hatred
    between fire and water.

The sympathy between a bum and a drug addict is
like the sympathy between a light bulb and a
burned-out light bulb.

Oscar Marcilla

Gravity—Love is like gravity pulling a divorced
couple together because when we separate we are
pulled together again.
Morning dew—love is like a soft morning dew which
has a magic formula which makes love appear.
Forgive and forget

Love=2 planets joining to make an eclipse
Love=a rocket ship going to the moon, when the
astronaut sees Venus the capsule goes crazy and
hits Venus's shadow and what an ugly Venus—
the ship takes off to earth.

Miklos Lengyel

The two love birds were in love.
When they were afraid, they always said, "Wow!"
They were like two bulbs—when it was dark, they
always kissed.
One day they blew each other's circuit
So they hugged and hugged and hugged, then kissed.

Hipolito Rivera

The love of the earth pulling the moon to it.
The love of a seed reaching for the sky.
The love of two kissing fish kissing each other.
The love of a tiny plant growing next to a tree.
The love of grass growing next to each other.
The love of two clouds going into each other.

Guy Peters

Two People Together

Two people together is like a clik clak
Two people together is like two pins standing in a
    bowling alley.
Two people together is like 88 together.
Two people together is like a chair and a desk.
Two people together is like two pins standing in a
    bowling alley—the ball is the mother, the alley is
    the father, and the children are pool tables.

Victor Drago

The Love Comparison

Two people in love are like two rockets blasting off to
    the same planet.
Two people in love are like the two of them floating
    free of gravity.
Two people in love are like light against light, all
    becoming as one.
Two people in love are like two stars put together
    turning into one planet.
Love is like thunder and lightning going through one
    planet.

Love is like two planets turning into the size of stars,
then becoming as one.

Arnaldo Gomez

Leaving someone is like an engine battery running
out.
Meeting someone is like the sun meeting the moon.
Moving away is like a heart full of sadness and tears.
Knowing nothing is like a bug full of bugs.
Kissing together is like Spring turning into a rainbow
of colors.
Two people in love is like two planets falling into
heaven.
Writing is like turning the earth upside down.
And saying good-bye is going to be like two strings
untying themselves into the blue blue yonder of
the silver-white moon.

Mayra Morales

Chapter Four

WILLIAM SHAKESPEARE

Three Songs

Come Unto These Yellow Sands

Come unto these yellow sands,
    And then take hands:
Court'sied when you have, and kiss'd,—
    The wild waves whist—
Foot it featly here and there;
And, sweet sprites, the burthen bear.
        Hark, hark!
            Bow, wow,
        The watch-dogs bark:
            Bow, wow.
Hark, hark! I hear
The strain of strutting chanticleer
Cry, Cock-a-diddle-dow!

—from *The Tempest*

Fancy

Tell me where is Fancy bred,
    Or in the heart or in the head?
How begot, how nourishèd?
    Reply, reply.
It is engender'd in the eyes;
With gazing fed; and Fancy dies

In the cradle where it lies.
   Let us all ring Fancy's knell:
   I'll begin it,—Ding, dong, bell!
All. Ding, dong, bell!

—from *The Merchant of Venice*

Where the Bee Sucks

Where the bee sucks, there suck I:
   In a cowslip's bell I lie;
There I couch when owls do cry.
On the bat's back I do fly
After summer merrily:
   Merrily, merrily, shall I live now,
   Under the blossom that hangs on the bough.

—from *The Tempest*

Songs

Many of Shakespeare's Songs appeal to children's sense of fantasy. They like the magical places and the wonderful creatures so small and light that they can sleep, like Ariel, in the cup of a flower. Along with the fantasy there is a fresh and sensuous feeling for nature, especially for its colors and sounds. The cowslips and bluebells are real, fresh flowers, yet invite the wildest and freest imaginings. The bird, animal, and object noises (Bow-wow, Cock-a-diddle-dow, and Ding, Dong, Bell) give a freedom and craziness to the poems which add to the feeling of gaiety and escape from restrictions and rules.

Several poetry ideas occurred to me, but the one I settled on was an Invitation Poem, based on "Come Unto These Yellow Sands." Given the beautiful sounds and colors of the Songs and the pleasure children find in inviting and in being invited, it seemed a good idea to have them write this: a poem in which you invite people (or only one person if you wish) to a magical beautiful place full of sounds and colors, and where all kinds of marvelous things may happen. In each line of your invitation you may want to put one sound or color, or maybe more. They found the idea of an invitation exciting, and, after we had exchanged a few ideas about where people might be invited, they began to write.

My students wrote invitations to "the land of freedom," to strange gardens full of music, to a country where everything is made of glass, to journeys through the air and over mountains; other invitations were to run through fields and feel the grass on one's feet, to hear the noises of the jungle, to go to the bottom of the sea, to visit a single red rose; others were "joke poems," invitations to be drowned or to visit the valley of the monsters. The most noticeable theme is desire for a place where one can be free—free from school, free from being forced to live in the city and to stay indoors, free to kiss and to love, free to do exactly as one likes.

Many of the poems have a nice songlike music, some with rhyme and some without. I usually discouraged my students from using rhyme, since it tended to restrict the expression of their thoughts and feelings, but in the Songs the sound is so central that it seemed all right to let them try to have the meaning—the thoughts and feelings—grow out of the sound or even be subordinate to it. I didn't ask them to use rhyme but didn't propose they not use it either. Some poems use it beautifully at the end of lines, like Carmen's and Maria Gutierrez's. Rosa's poem has fine rhymes inside the lines. Other poems seemed to catch the delicate music of Shakespeare's Songs without rhyme—the first four lines of Chip's poem, for example; and the poems by Lynne and Valerie.

One might wish to dramatize a little the sensuous sounds in the Songs to help get the children in a dreamy, playful, and imaginative mood. They can close their eyes and listen to ordinary sounds—a whistle, a book slammed shut, a ruler striking an empty glass—and say what words those sounds are like, what things they remind them of, what colors the sounds have. Or a teacher can bring a toy trumpet to school, a silvery-sounding bell, a recorder, a violin or a guitar, or a record of Elizabethan music, or a record of object or animal sounds. Such mechanical aids shouldn't overwhelm Shakespeare, of course; they should be used sparingly, just enough to make the children excited about their senses and wanting to write. Two or three toots on a toy trumpet might be enough, or a half-minute or so of listening to a record.

If one wishes to stay with Shakespeare's Songs awhile, there are others that are good to teach, such as the "Over Hill, over Dale" song, "Under the Greenwood Tree," "Aubade," and "Orpheus with His Lute Made Trees." Another kind of Invitation Poem children might like is Yeats's "Who Goes with Fergus?"

The last two fifth-grade poems and the two seventh-grade poems in this section are by students at the Friends' School in North Dartmouth, Massachusetts.

FIFTH GRADE

Travel with me over the golden garden and hear the
    daisies go daie, daie, with gay.
We shall fly over beautiful skies where there's
    freedom that goes ding, ding, ding, dong.
We are free, free, come, come, I am inviting you to
    the land of freedom where dogs go quack, quack,
    instead of bow, wow, bark, bark.
Where everything is different in mixed colors red,
    yellow, pink, bluish blue.
Oh come, come to my invitation to the land of
    freedom and let's be free forever. Oh diddle,
    diddle dee.

Rosa Rosario

Will you come with me in the woods and hear the
    birds chirp, the bees buzz, buzz, and the rabbit
    going hopity, hop, hop.
Come with me in the jungle and hear the lions roar,
    snakes stt, stt, and Tarzan saying ah ah ah
    (banging on his chest).

Lynne Reiff

Come with me where the rainbow dies.
Come with me where the birds fly, where the wind
    goes wiz, wiz.
I will take my loved one there, where the wind goes
    zerrr, zerrr!

Stephen Lenik

Come With Me

Come with me to the bottom of the sea and you'll
    hear the fishes go gulp! gulp!
And see the swordfish have a duel and the seahorses
    race and go click! clack! click clack and the
    rainbows sing.

Valerie Goodall

When I fly with you I hear a honk honk in my ear,
    but when we stop I hear a ring-a-ling in me
When I walk with you, you make the bear go
    sing-a-ding.
When we talk close I go weeeeeeee.

Richard Rivera

Come with me to the edge of the river—if they come
    to us and bother us, push them in the river, and
    if I try to kiss you from lips to lips and cry all I
    can.

Damary Hernandez

Come with me to a red rose
Come with me through the wind
To a little red rose
That's been there all the time
Ding, dong, the bells so ring
Ding, dong, the bells so not ring.

Chip Wareing

Up up and away, come with me and let's fly away to
      the heavens and we'll have fun together playing,
      kissing, and running in the sky together. We'll
      have fun, I'm sure of it, kissing in the sky.

Benny Vincifora

Come and sing and laugh and play in this lovely
      garden, where the sun shines every day, in this
      lovely garden.
Where the kids laugh and play, everybody feels so
      gay, come and sing and laugh and play, in this
      lovely garden.

Carmen Aponte

Friends, friends, come with me.
Go to a wonderful place that has birds and trees all
      around
Birds are singing and trees are playing beautiful
      music.

So come with me to the wonderful place with all
  your friends.
So enjoy yourself to sing with the birds, and dance
  with your nice friends.
Come with me to a wonderful place.

Yuk Leung

Invitation

Oh come with me to see a Daisy, lah lah and it is a
  yellow and all shades of it and Ding Dong Dee.
If someone bothers us, stick a pin on their seat and
  soon and 15 thumb tacks so they will jump up.
And put a lion on the chair and let teacher sit on it
  because she gave us 115 spelling words and 100
  examples.
And say you're sorry for what you did so seriously be
  good and all the time practice instruments and
  let her give no homework for the rest of the year.
  Okay.
I *mean it*. O.K. and surprise her every time and say
  surprise.
And the invitation is for the 5–2 only.

Andrea Dockery

Come with me to the land of glass where everything
  is so gleamy that you can pass.
But when you sing la la la the glass will pass.
And when you meet a lady don't bow or you will pass
  like the glass.

Don't try to relax on the ground for it's too slippery
    cause it's made of wax and glass.
You can't eat anything, for food is made of yellow
    wax and glass.
But when you are out you are free as a bird or glass.

Fung Ping Lui

Come with me to a grassy field.
We will take off our shoes
And run in the grass
And it will tickle our toes.

Melissa Blitz

Come away with me,
I'll carry you over my knee.
We'll have lots of fun, we'll bathe in the sun under
    the old apple tree.
We'll fly away, over mountains and hills.
And then for us the world will stand still.
The world will be at our command and finally we
    will land.
I'll ring the doorbell, ding-a-ling
And as I leave, you will sing,
"I'll be ready when the doorbell rings."

Maria Gutierrez

Come with me to the American flag
We can go to the first star on it
We can jump from star to star and stitch to stitch
We go boing, beznock as we bounce
We can walk on the stripes
Then climb on the pole all the way to the golden top
We can slide down the pole and zoom by the red,
    white and blue
We can walk on the air, or fly on a bird's back
Then we can go to the beach and climb big sea shells
    and big sea rocks
We have to be careful when it comes to the ocean, or
    we might fall in and be lost forever
I hope you can come
We can sleep on leaves and use grass for pillows
Tell a stork to tell me if you can come.

Karen Shapiro

Come with me to planet Roe
You take a left at Mars then go straight ahead to
    Pluto
From Pluto you go right to Neptune
Then go right under Neptune to planet Roe
We will go inside and look and talk to the screech
    men
They will say hello like this
    screeeeeeeeeeeeeeeeeeeeeeeeecccchhh
A screech man has eight feet, three eyes, two heads
    and nose that is eighteen feet long
They are six inches tall and have green faces
We will leave at 109 o'clock

Meet me at the sun and I will pick you up with my
    flying chimney
Be there

Mike McGuill

SEVENTH GRADE

Come into the tree with no leaves
I will be there listening to the hooting of an owl
Woodpeckers tapping on the bark outside—tap, tap,
    bang
The black colored starling comes in to make a nest
Red squirrels walk up and down a tree making a soft
    pitter patter
When night comes again everything is dark black.

Edward Siegal

Follow the foot prints
Come follow, come follow
And reach a glass fence
All with gay colors
Of scarlet, blue and yellow
Up the glass step you go
And hear the light wind blow
Wwhhit, wwhhit is flutter
Of the glazed bird beside

The willie wolly and
Conky conka
And don't forget
To find me in the
Queeny flower.

Marcy Snow

Chapter Five

WALT WHITMAN

from *Song of Myself*

(sections 1 and 2)

1

I celebrate myself,
And what I assume you shall assume,
For every atom belonging to me as good belongs to
    you.

I loafe and invite my soul,
I lean and loafe at my ease. . . . observing a spear of
    summer grass.

2

Houses and rooms are full of perfumes. . . . the
    shelves are crowded with perfumes,
I breathe the fragrance myself, and know it and like
    it,
The distillation would intoxicate me also, but I shall
    not let it.

The atmosphere is not a perfume. . . . it has no taste
    of the distillation. . . . it is odorless,
It is for my mouth forever. . . . I am in love with it,
I will go to the bank by the wood and become
    undisguised and naked,
I am mad for it to be in contact with me.

The smoke of my own breath,
Echoes, ripples, and buzzed whispers. . . . loveroot,
    silkthread, crotch and vine,

My respiration and inspiration. . . . the beating of my
    heart. . . . the passing of blood and air through
    my lungs,
The sniff of green leaves and dry leaves, and of the
    shore and darkcolored sea-rocks, and of hay in
    the barn,
The sound of the belched words of my voice. . . .
    words loosed to the eddies of the wind,

A few light kisses. . . . a few embraces. . . . reaching
    around of arms,
The play of shine and shade on the trees as the
    supple boughs wag,
The delight alone or in the rush of the streets, or
    along the fields and hillsides
The feeling of health. . . . the full-noon trill. . . . the
    song of me rising from bed and meeting the sun.

Have you reckoned a thousand acres much? Have you
    reckoned the earth much?
Have you practiced so long to learn to read?
Have you felt so proud to get at the meaning of
    poems?

Stop this day and night with me and you shall
    possess the origin of all poems,
You shall possess the good of the earth and sun. . . .
    there are millions of suns left,
You shall no longer take things at second or third
    hand. . . . nor look through the eyes of the dead.
    . . . nor feed on the spectres in books,
You shall not look through my eyes either, nor take
    things from me,
You shall listen to all sides and filter them from
    yourself.

from *Song of Myself*

(sections 1 and 2)

"Song of Myself" is appealing to children because it offers them secret knowledge and power in a fresh, friendly, breezy, almost Santa-Clausy kind of way. Whitman says "I'm terrific, and you're terrific too. Come along with me and we'll see and do great things!" His tone is a combination of boasting and open-hearted generosity—"I know it all, and I'm going to share it with you!" And that Whitman says this kind of secret knowledge he has is better than what is found in books is of course refreshing to children reading it in school. Children can identify rather easily with Whitman's claim to have important secret knowledge: they know things which are obviously important, which adults apparently don't know (though Whitman seems to)—how to be close to animals and other creatures and to nature, how beautiful the world is, and how exciting and endless it is to be alive in it.

For the poetry idea I told the children to suppose that they knew secrets which gave them a special power and to write a poem in which, in a boasting, generous, and secret-telling kind of way, they offer to share these secrets. I gave and asked for examples of some kinds of things people could know— what it is like under the ocean, why the sky is blue, what the rain hears, what the grass and stones say. But secrets are secrets, and I told the children to keep the best secrets for themselves and for their poems.

They wrote about secret knowledge and special powers of many kinds. The reader is invited to the other side of the moon, to the world of secrets, to the inside of a flower, "up to the path to nowhere," into dreams, and to a "world of our own to live the way we want." He is offered knowledge of how things really are beneath surface appearances, of where to find out about things, of the origins of things, of the history of the world, of the nature of happiness, of the reason for human cruelty, and of how it feels to be hurt. Some poems, like Rafael's, were mainly about a superhero kind of power; others, like Vivien's and Marion's, about escaping into a place free of restrictions and cares. The familiar childhood idea of a "special secret place" where certain things can be seen appears in quite a few of the poems.

A Whitman-like use of speech-making repetition and rhetoric appears in some of the poems. A few children picked up Whitman's "plain-talking" and sometimes rather "smart-alecky" tone, too—"This is not a side show, don't be mistaken . . ." (Tracy); "Do you know how to get to the end of the universe? I do. If you don't, you won't find it in the almanac . . ." (Lisa).

There are other sections of "Song of Myself" that would be as good to teach as these—section 15, for example, the great list beginning "The pure contralto," or section 26 about the sounds the poet hears. Parts of these sections could be read to children along with sections 1 and 2 to give them more ideas. Whichever part of the poem a teacher chooses, I would suggest it be one which is suffused with Whitman's big breezy sensuousness, secrecy, and power, for I think that is the quality of his poetry that speaks to children most. I would suggest not teaching the frequently used "What Is Grass" episode in section 6 of the poem, which, if taken by itself, lacks this quality.

SIXTH GRADE

What I Know

Come with me to the other side of the moon.
I'll tell you where the moon comes from.
And where we come from
Where the sky came from

Come with me
This is not a side show, don't be mistaken
I can open the world with my brain, and yours can
    do it too. COME WITH ME. . . .

Tracy Lahab

A Flower to Go To

Come with me to a flower.
I know I can get there and it's a beautiful place.
It's the insides of a flower—it's beautiful especially if
    you and I are going to share it.
We'll go there tonight at twilight, we'll meet there
    when the sky is orange and the moon is pink.
    We'll go in,
And ask one another questions and love this secret
    place of love.

Vivien Tuft

Come With Me

Come with me and I'll show you my heart. I know
    where it is. I know all about it.
Come with me to a place I know. It's a very
    mysterious place. I get there through the back
    roads of my mind.
Come with me, I'll take you to a world, not a world
    that you know. Not a world that I know. But a
    world that nobody knows, not me or you. It's a
    world of our own to live the way we want.

To do the things we want.
To know the things we want.
There's no way to get there.
It's ourselves that takes us there.

Vivien Tuft

Come with me to the world of secrets.
Do you know how a mind grows? I do. Do you? If you
    don't, you won't find it on a piece of paper, you'll
    find it on the dark blue sky.
Do you know how to get to the end of the universe? I
    do. If you don't, you won't find it in the almanac,
    you'll find it in the number nine.
Do you know where fish came from? I do. If you
    don't, you won't find it in a book about fish, you'll
    find it on the earth's equator.

Lisa Smalley

Fish

Do you know what—I'm half fish and half man
I look normal
But once I'm in the water
I turn gold
I turn and toss and talk to the fish
Why? I guess it's because I love the chilly blue green
    water
It's so silky

Once I get out I'm me again
I wish I was a fish all the time
No cares, no troubles, free of everything
Everything on earth

Marion Mackles

Come with me to my world of secrets.
One of my secrets is when the sun is shining on
    Manhattan, it's really a glittering star of
    darkness.
One of my secrets is when the stars are sparkling in
    the night, it is really a moon of brightness.
One of my secrets is that a little fly is really an
    enormous butterfly in feelings.

Jeannie Turner

Come With Me. . . .

Come with me and I'll show you a rabbit with no
    head.
Come with me on a mountain and I'll show you a live
    skeleton.
Come with me and I'll show you one million
    nothings.

Lorraine Fedison

Sunny Day

Come with me, I'll show a secret. The sun shines
    when I feel good, and if I don't, it will become
    breezy.

                                        Hipolito Rivera

Breezy, Breezy

Oh Breezy, Breezy, I'll show a secret to you. I am
    lucky, nuckled-headed.

                                        Hipolito Rivera

My Secrets Are Your Secrets

When I looked at a hole I thought I saw a dead lady.
Come with me, and I'll show you some jewels in a
    cave.
Come with me, and I'll show you a live animal in the
    museum.
But be sure to come with me and be sure not to tell
    anybody.
It's only a secret between you and me.

                                        Lorraine Fedison

The sky is filled with flying mermaids which are
    invisible to everyone but me.
But when you go underwater, all you can see is
    scuba-diving devils.

Billy Constant

One day, a nice warm day, I took a long swim
in a pool of water. I heard a voice! Whose voice
could it be? Then I looked up. I saw the moon's
face. I looked at it. I saw the mouth of the moon
say something and in a few minutes I had a
shock in the water. I could not understand the
moon's language, and in one minute I understood it—fantastic! I talked with the moon all
night. Then I went to bed. In the morning I went
to my friend's house. I told him to come and I
would teach him to talk with the moon too. So
then night came again. I went out to take a swim.
When the voice appeared I told my friend I
would teach him to talk with the moon, and in a
few minutes my friend talked with the moon. He
could not believe his ears, but I taught him to
speak moon language. I made money teaching
people to talk moon.

Miklos Lengyel

Come with Me into My World of Dreams

Come with me into my dreams and you shall
know everything I know. All my secrets shall be
yours, all my wisdom as well. No one has ever

entered. Please don't go, because you will be able
to fly or break through a wall or something.
Come with me, my friend and we shall go, but
please keep going with me. Here we're super-
men in this town. Sorry we can't stay, but we
have to keep going. There is the mind of tran-
quility and there was a hole where anyone can
get swallowed. There, it wasn't so bad, was it?
Well, good-bye, my friend.

Rafael Camacho

Close your eyes and follow me to the secret cave full
    of thought.
Only your thinking will give you answers.
The cave is full of the moon's red light and the star's
    purple glows.
In this cave lives the history of the world. The mind
    that lives in this cave belongs to everybody. It
    controls us.
Ask it questions and the answers will stick in your
    mind.
In the heavens above the moon lives God the creator
    from the beginning of time.

Andrew Vecchione

The Secret of My Soul

Follow me up the path to nowhere.
Where the sky is black, the moon is red, and where
    my soul lives. It's the place where all questions
    are answered.

How did the sheep get their wool?
How does the moon fade out in the breeze?
How do people kill and why do they kill?
How do people feel when they are hurt?
My soul carries these secrets that only I know.

Andrew Vecchione

Chapter Six

WALLACE STEVENS

Thirteen Ways of Looking at a Blackbird

I

Among twenty snowy mountains
The only moving thing
Was the eye of the blackbird.

2

I was of three minds,
Like a tree
In which there are three blackbirds.

3

The blackbird whirled in the autumn winds.
It was a small part of the pantomime.

4

A man and a woman
Are one.
A man and a woman and a blackbird
Are one.

5

I do not know which to prefer,
The beauty of inflections
Or the beauty of innuendoes.
The blackbird whistling
Or just after.

6

Icicles filled the long window
With barbaric glass
The shadow of the blackbird
Crossed it, to and fro.
The mood
Traced in the shadow
An indecipherable cause.

7

O thin men of Haddam,
Why do you imagine golden birds?
Do you not see how the blackbird
Walks around the feet
Of the women about you?

8

I know noble accents
And lucid, inescapable rhythms;
But I know, too,
That the blackbird is involved
In what I know.

9

When the blackbird flew out of sight,
It marked the edge
Of one of many circles.

10

At the sight of blackbirds
Flying in a green light,
Even the bawds of euphony
Would cry out sharply.

11

He rode over Connecticut
In a glass coach.
Once, a fear pierced him,
In that he mistook
The shadow of his equipage
For blackbirds.

12

The river is moving.
The blackbird must be flying.

13

It was evening all afternoon.
It was snowing
And it was going to snow.
The blackbird sat
In the cedar-limbs.

WALLACE STEVENS

(AMERICAN, 1879–1955)

Thirteen Ways of Looking at a Blackbird

The gamelike quality of this poem is appealing to children: How many ways can you see a blackbird? They enjoy seeing the blackbird in all the different ways Stevens describes it— for example as part of a story (in stanzas 8 and 11), as part of a stage show (stanza 3), as part of what sounds like a sermon or other serious speech (stanza 7), as part of a math problem (stanzas 4 and 9), as just a very tiny detail in a huge, silent landscape (first and last stanzas). Seeing the blackbird in all these ways is intriguing in itself and gives the children exciting ideas of different ways of talking about things in their own poems.

The poetry idea was, "Write a poem in which you talk about the same thing in a number of different ways." I added, "Be sure you think about how it really looks or seems for each thing you say about it." I said they could, if they liked, put a different way of seeing it in every line. I suggested, too, that the thing they write about be a fairly ordinary thing, such as Stevens considers the blackbird to be.

I suggested some subjects they might like to write about— objects in the classroom or other things they might have had a number of thoughts and fantasies about: the window, a pen, the blackboard, an animal, a bird, a flower, a shirt or dress. I asked them for suggestions, too. Then we tried out a few ways of looking at something—how does a window look? how many windows make a house? or a mansion? what's big as a window? what else can you see through? do you know secrets about a window? in what way is a glass window more beautiful than a window made of gold? what's a story about a window?

Along with having the pleasure of describing the same thing in different ways, the children can get from Stevens's poem the pleasant and interesting experience of looking at something very concentratedly until it really does begin to look strange to them and to suggest other things.

It might be good to dramatize the situation somewhat by bringing some ordinary yet beautiful thing, like a small animal or a fruit or vegetable, to school for the children to look at and touch before they try to write about it in as many ways as they can. I had found out before that the physical presence of something unusual can inspire children to write. At Muse, in Bedford-Stuyvesant, where I taught for a while, the children wrote wonderful things while observing rabbits and mice. Once at PS 61, when as a part of a regular writing lesson, I brought some oranges and lemons and ears of corn to school, and passed them around and asked the children to look at them and touch and smell them as if they didn't know what they were, and write poems about what they thought they were; there were some extremely vivid images, like Vivien Tufts's description of an orange as the earth, with "all the Greek myths" inside it, and Tommy Rogaski's vision of an ear of corn as a "funny typewriter" with "green hair." This kind of wild imagining was actually made possible by the real, plain object being there. And maybe, too, the fact that all the children were looking at and thinking about the same things made those things seem more exciting.

There are many other Stevens poems about ways of seeing and imagining things. One children would especially like, I think, is this section of his poem "Someone Puts a Pineapple Together," which is a list of twelve different things or scenes the poet sees when he looks at a pineapple. Of course, having a real-life something for the children to look at in this case would be very desirable. Perhaps a pineapple to help explain the poem, and oranges or artichokes to inspire the children's own. One could ask the children to close their eyes tight each time and forget what they were supposed to be seeing, then open them suddenly, look at the orange or whatever, and write down just what they saw, no matter how crazy. Their visions are unlikely to be much crazier than Stevens's visions of the pineapple—

1. The hut stands by itself beneath the palms.
2. Out of their bottle the green genii come.
3. A vine has climbed the other side of the wall.

4. The sea is spouting upward out of rocks.
5. The symbol of feasts and of oblivion . . .
6. White sky, pink sun, trees on a distant peak.

7. These lozenges are nailed-up lattices.
8. The owl sits humped. It has a hundred eyes.
9. The cocoanut and cockerel in one.

10. This is how yesterday's volcano looks.
11. There is an island Palahude by name—
12. An uncivil shape like a gigantic haw.

Children will probably especially enjoy the view of the pineapple as a hut, as an owl, and as yesterday's volcano, and also Stevens's comparing it to a sound—Haw!—a big fat sound that resembles a pineapple. This pineapple passage might in fact be a better work of Stevens to teach younger children than "Thirteen Ways of Looking at a Blackbird," since it is more purely visual. But both poems have their virtues.

One rule a teacher can suggest to make the lessons with Stevens's poems more dramatic and strange is that children not use "is like" or "looks like," and that except in the title they not even name the object they are talking about. This would mean saying to describe an orange, for instance, "The tennis ball is on fire," instead of "The orange looks like a tennis ball that is on fire."

Sarah Spongberg, teaching seventh- and ninth-grade students, devoted three class sessions to "Thirteen Ways of Looking at a Blackbird." When students show they are very interested, consecutive lessons on a poem may be a good idea.

FIFTH GRADE

The Color of Black

When I was looking at Carmen's pen, it was black, it
    moved back and forth, left and right, up and
    down.
It seems like a cold winter night when it was dark
    outside and everyone fell asleep and everyone
    had a beautiful dream.
It seems like a boy got a black eye.
It seems like I saw Mr. Koch's black hair.
It seems like I am in a fire drill and it seems like a
    group of blackbirds are going on a trip.

Yuk Leung

I was looking at Yuk's airplane sharpener when I
    thought that it had a name
Its name was XSP and its number is 550
Also it was a dark red. It was red because it bumped
    into a rainbow.
It was beautiful. It had a hatch.
The sharpener was yellow.
When the hatch opened it turned into a crane or a
    submarine.
Then it just flew away.
Good-bye, airplane.

Carmen Berrios

The Four Thinker Ring

1. My ring makes me think of Valentine's Day.
2. I had this ring for a long time.
3. When I wear it, it makes me think of my heart, because it is shaped like a heart.
4. My ring makes me think of a day in the winter when it's snowing very hard and people are happy.

Lynne Reiff

There are three ways of looking at a paper boat
    floating in a lake with my friend in it and sailing
    away
The boat went to my mind because I did not know
    what it would do. It would be terrible if it
    crashed it would be my only hope my inspiration
    to make me content.

Rebecca Crespo

Four Ways of Looking at Scissors

When I look at scissors I see people dancing.
When I look at scissors I can see a piece of paper
    being cut.
When I look at a broken branch, I can see a scissors.

Valerie Goodall

I

The rose is pink with things in pink

2

If you take a rose and smell the rose with pink it will
    smell you and will turn you pink in a rose

3

If you smell a rose it will not have air to smell unless
    you stop smelling it

Damary Hernandez

A watch on a cold day looks like two sticks running
    after each other.

Melissa Blitz

Daisies

I walk through a field of green and see a piece of
    gold in a field of white.
I had the best gold in the world—Daisies.
My friend gave me a flower. It was daisies and in his
    hand daisies are the best.

Antoinette Anderson

I see Jose as a romantic singer.
I see Jose as a wild girl-chaser.
He doesn't only chase girls, but faints for them.

Richard Ulloa

Two Ways of Looking at a Rose

A rose is like thirteen-hundred rose petals dropped
    into the water and floating away & away & away
    & away far away.
A rose is like a baby's gentle skin and I was its
    mother. I put it in water so it wouldn't die. I
    called her rosepetal.

Ana Perez

My pen looks like a torpedo when you turn it
    sideways and the hook is on top.

Benny Vincifora

Four Ways of Looking at a Wolf

A wolf in a book looks like a growly dog that is wild.
A werewolf and Frankenstein put together is a wolf.
A wolf is like Godzila when he has a stomach ache.
A wolf is like a hippie growing hair.

Joseph Scifo

My pen is like a machine that runs and runs and
    never stops,
My pen ink is like a purse of gold.
My pen is like a poem-writer.
My pen is like a human being.
My pen is like the Empire State Building.
My pen is like a man.
My pen is like a pen that never erases.

Richard Rivera

The Three Ways to Look into an Enchanted Mirror

1. To look and see your true identity the true and
   the false the trick of eternity
2. To see a snow-covered mountain.
3. To know that you saw more of you than ever.

Chip Wareing

4 Ways to Look at a Top

A top is like a person dancing.
A top is like a person and King Kong—it is like when
    a top is spinning and the top is really a person
    and King Kong picks the top that is the person
    up.
A top is like a person when it gets split or cut.
A top is like a person getting laid up.

Wilson Perez

Ten Ways of Looking at Roses

The rose opened like a road to colorful dreams.
Roses are like a place of kingdom.
Looking at a rose is like seeing beauty after an ugly
    day.
The rose is like a sign of hope, nature, and beauty.
Looking at a rose is looking at a new, colorful world.
The rose has a look of living forever and ever.
Looking at a rose is like seeing the first thing in a
    hundred years.
The rose is nature's way of looking at things.

Rosa Rosario

SEVENTH GRADE

5 Ways of Looking at a Cloud

The grayish white fluff soft as a
Marshmallow made into a giant pillow
Against the blue sky

A white dove flying across the sky
Dropping its downy white feathers
As it goes

A cotton ball that someone has
Dropped against the blue field

A white rabbit jumped across the
Sky and lost its soft fluffy tail

When my grandmother starts knitting
And she leaves a ball of yarn—

Pam Wild

5 Ways of Looking at a Pond

A pond is just a mirror
                left alone, amongst the grasses
                to reflect the sky

A single tear from skies above

finally cooled
by evening winds

A shiny silver button
                dropped from a giant's coat
                never to be found

Made of green jade
                a chinese bowl
                surrounded by leafy, green temples

Blue paint accidentally dribbled
                on the green carpet
                of a hill.

Molly Hankwitz

NINTH GRADE

Five Ways of Looking at a Flower

1

Sitting on a chair
Among gray buildings
Is a flower.

2

People of New York
Imagine the country?
Can they see a flower
On a crowded subway?

3

Waving wind
Moving a small plant
A bright shining sun
Paints the shadow of a large flower.

4

A flower is embedded
My thoughts are with it
So are an insect's.

5

The flower wilted to the ground,
It was the finish of many things.

Martin Jacobvitz

Chapter Seven

WILLIAM CARLOS WILLIAMS

This Is Just to Say

I have eaten
the plums
that were in
the icebox

and which
you were probably
saving
for breakfast

Forgive me
they were delicious
so sweet
and so cold

The Locust Tree in Flower

Among
of
green

stiff
old
bright

broken
branch
come

white
sweet
May

again

Between Walls

the back wings
of the

hospital where
nothing

will grow lie
cinders

in which shine
the broken

pieces of a green
bottle

WILLIAM CARLOS WILLIAMS

(AMERICAN, 1883–1963)

This Is Just to Say;
The Locust Tree in Flower; Between Walls

I taught these three poems in one class, having the children write poems with each. The lesson moved along quickly and turned out to be a very rich and interesting one. It was the children who set the pace for it; I had come to class thinking I would have time to teach one, or at the most two of the poems. But they were excited by them all and seemed in a mood to write one poem after another. The Williams poems are, in fact, simple and, if presented in the right way, extremely appealing to children. Once they knew what a poem was about, they wanted to write. The hour was busy but it didn't seem rushed. The very fact that they wrote so many poems (some children wrote six or seven) in one hour seemed to add to their feeling of inspiration and freedom and to put them in a fairly wild and receptive creative mood. Themes and techniques were carried over from one poem to the next, and the excitement of having written one poem became a creative excitement for writing the next one.

I began by giving everyone the three poems to read, then talked about them a little. One reason I'd decided to teach them was to give my students an example of a poet who wrote in ordinary language about ordinary things, so I talked about that. Also, I asked them if they liked the short lines, and if they liked the poem being so small and about just one thing. In fact, they did—the shortness and simplicity of the poems gave them the special pleasure of being able to think of an entire poem at once— a poem that could be written quickly, a single statement with only one or two words in a line.

I began with "This Is Just to Say," which has a theme children find irresistible, and which I used for the poetry idea, apologizing for something you're really secretly glad you did. Apologizing was a new note in their poetry (as inviting had been in the Shakespeare poems) and they enjoyed it; they enjoyed, too, asserting the importance of their secret pleasure against the world of adult regulations. They apologized, and were pleased about, breaking things, taking things, forgetting and neglecting things, eating things, hitting people, and looking at things.

After they had finished these poems, I collected them and read a few aloud. Then I went on to "The Locust Tree in Flower," concentrating in that poem on its form: the use of one-word lines, and the disjointedness—the poem isn't a sentence but a series of individual words used somewhat like brushstrokes in a painting: each word adds something to what one sees, but it's not till near the end that one knows what the whole picture is. To make sure the children understood how this worked, I had them do a class collaboration. I stood at the blackboard and wrote down the words they called out to me to be lines for the poem. There was a sort of informal vote on each word (line). If we didn't like it, I asked for other suggestions. The children were delighted with this activity, and wanted to go on to another class poem, but I asked them to write poems of their own. The poetry idea was to write a poem about something you see, with one word in every line. I asked the children to try not to make the poem a sentence but to make it jagged like "The Locust Tree in Flower."

Excited by the collaboration and the idea of one word per line, the children wrote quickly and well. Some poems had vividness of a kind I hadn't seen in even their best Comparison Poems—Andrew's about Coke, for example; Guy's about a dandelion; Jorge's about a wheel; and Miklos's "Beauty of the World" and Vivien's "Thunder in the Sky," which used Williams's techniques on a somewhat more complex kind of subject matter. The one-word-at-a-time brushstroke technique freed them from the burden of complete sentences and helped them to see and write about things sharply and freshly.

After collecting and reading a few of these poems, I asked the children if they felt up to another one. They said yes, so we did "Between Walls." What I concentrated on here was the un-beautifulness of the broken glass bottle and how Williams thinks it is beautiful anyway. I had chosen this poem because even more clearly than the other two it could point the children away from "highly poetical" things, like palaces and snowcapped mountains, as the only proper ones to write poetry about. It could help them to look for what was beautiful to them in the things they really saw. The poetry idea was, "Write a poem about something not supposed to be beautiful but which you really secretly think is, the way Williams thinks the glass behind the hospital is beautiful." I asked them for examples, to be sure they were thinking about really plain things. They wrote about the beauty of tin cans, charcoal, glass, a shining broken vase, garbage, a paper cup torn into little pieces.

There were various carry-overs from one poem to another—one-word-a-line apologies, for example, and the use of the "Locust Tree" brushstroke technique in the ugly-beautiful poems, such as Jorge's about the can. All three Williams poems carry a sense of the brightness and beauty of plain things and of a plain way of talking about them. They reinforce each other, and the children got a lot, I think, from having them all together. One thing was a new feeling for what a line of poetry was and for going from one line to another without completing a statement.

The sixth-grade students I happened to teach Williams to had been enthusiastically writing poetry for several years, and so felt free about writing and had a great many ideas. Not every group of students will be able to work that hard at poetry for an hour. A good class could be made out of any one or two of these poems

Short poems have an obvious appeal for children and suggest easy and pleasant things for them to write. Of those I know, I think these and a few others by Williams are among the best to teach them. Haiku are widely used as a poetry model for children (some are included in the anthology). If haiku are used, I'd suggest ignoring their restrictive syllable count and de-emphasizing their often remote subject matter: snowy slopes, delicate bamboo shoots, shimmering pools, and other things most school children don't get to see much of. Williams's short poems give children the haiku-like pleasure of short lines without the haiku-like restrictions, and they suggest as subjects things which are a regular part of their lives.

SIXTH GRADE

1   This Is Just to Say

Dear Dog

Please
for
give
me
for
eating
your
dog
biscuit.

      Lorraine Fedison

Dear Biscuit

I'm
so
sorry
for
taking
you
away
from

your
friend
the
Dog.

Mayra Morales

This Is Just To Say

Thank you for the ants you put in my bed.
This is just to say thank you for giving me the purple
    sunset on my birthday.

Andrew Vecchione

Sorry But It Was Beautiful

Sorry I took your money and burned it but it looked
    like the world falling apart when it crackled and
    burned.
So I think it was worth it after all you can't see the
    world fall apart every day.

Andrew Vecchione

Sorry and Good

I
Dropped
a
glass

Nice
and
Sparkling
color
but
sorry
I
am
and
Glad
I
am
too.

Vilma Mejias

Dear Cat

Please
for
give
me
for
watching
your
eyes
gleam
in
the
night.

Lorraine Fedison

This Is Just to Say

That the dog
tore your
shoes in
to little pieces
and I let him
do it. It was quite amusing.

Vivien Tuft

Dear Bird

I am sorry
To kill you
But when you're cooked
You taste too good
With gravy.

Author unknown

The Red Flag

I
am
sorry
I
have
eaten
a
red
a
blue
a

white?
flag
but
I
ate
cause
I
was
hungry.

Miklos Lengyel

The Golden Fleece I Ate

me:	dear	god:	dear
	god		boy
	forgive		who
	me		ate
	for		my
	eating		golden
	the		fleece
	golden		I
	fleece		shall
	Thou		punish
	sent		Thee
	down		by
	to		making
	save		you
	Rolmus		save
	and		Rolmus
	Ramous		and
			Ramous

Miklos Lengyel

This is just to say
I have taken the eggs
Of the bird's nest
But I didn't have
Any sense that the
Mother bird is looking
For its children and
Worried. I am sorry
Mother bird and I shall
Return them when they
Hatch. I just couldn't see
Them out there in the
Cold Weather.

Hector Figueroa

I didn't mean it.
I'm sorry, but it was so good.
I didn't know it was going to be in the apple pie.
I'm sorry. I won't do it anymore.

Victor Drago

I Just Want to Say

I have eaten
The flowers
That were
On your head
Which you
Were probably
Saving for

A funeral
Please forgive
Me.
I liked to say
You looked great
In a coffin
I'll bury you
For what I did
Please forgive me

Rafael Camacho

2   The Locust Tree in Flower

Rose

Among
its
ground
lies
petals
red
small
thorns
green

*Collaboration poem
by the sixth-grade class*

Thunder in Sky

Among
  morning
    sky
      myself
    sees
      pink
      white

blue
      cotton
      clouds
    thunder
      rain
        me.

Vivien Tuft

The Grass

Among
the
ground
lies
green
small
grass

Lorraine Fedison

The Colored Color

I
saw
a
pink
orange
purple
black
green
colored
color

Lorraine Fedison

The Bird

sky
clouds
wings
gray
up
down
flap
flip

Marion Mackles

The Bud

Among
its
house
lies
thorns
black and
brown.

Hipolito Rivera

Among
the
tree
is
thee
in
love
with
a
man
with
the
face
of
a
dog.

Ileana Mesen

Dandelion

around
the
body
lies
fur
which
is
on
top
of
a
stem
whch
is
all
yellow.

Guy Peters

The Lovely Rabbit

Pink
yellow
Pink
fluffy
creature
down
chewing
milk
hoppy
scratch
tomorrow

Mayra Morales

The Cop

He
is
in
a
blue
uniform
and
a
shiny
badge
and
black

shoes
he
is
The
Cop

Victor Drago

Clouds

Sky
      Blue
Dawn
      orange
Beauty
      love
Shine
      Bye
RAIN!

Tracy Lahab

Poem

Among
the
sky
I
see
a
bird

and
it
said
tweet
tweet

      Daniel Lacey

Fear

I
feared
my
Shadow
But
It
was
nice
to
see
myself
in
fear.

      Vilma Mejias

Mother Nature

Among
the
brown
tall

tree
lies
a
bird
with
little
infants
of
its
own.

Vilma Mejias

The Beauty of the World

among
Mr.
Bowman
many
its
things
live
green,
blue
is
world.

Miklos Lengyel

Coke

Among
water
lies
sun
purple
green
red
coke
splatters
in
water
like
petals
on
roses
floating
in
the
sun
set
of
the
world

Andrew Vecchione

Greenbird

Among
its
feet
lie

feathers
green
pointed
beak
chirps
a
song
on
the
willow tree
it
is
a
greenbird

Lisa Smalley

Love

sex
mouth
touch
dream
wink
smile
peek
rose
feels
good

Author unknown

The Rolling Wheel

Among
the
cement
wheels
chains
Ride
with
slowness
and
turns

Jorge Robles

3 Between Walls

The Deserted Road

There was a very old deserted road
I took a walk on it,
And all of a sudden I saw the most beautiful thing
That I had ever seen on this road.
A paper cup torn into little pieces.

Vivien Tuft

The Charcoal

Inside the base-
ment

where there
is no beauty

lies a piece
of crumbled
up black

dark charcoal
shining from the

flaming fire
and soon to
join the fire

Rafael Camacho

The Dirty Can

Along
the
street
rolls
an
old

crumbled
shining
with
beauty
a
can

Rafael Camacho

The ticking of the clock
Came from the wall above
Filled with bricks and wood.
The sound of a broken dish filled the air.

Jeannie Turner

Goldglass

In the back yard
Lies in the sun
White glass
Reflecting the sun

Marion Mackles

Nothing Made to Something

The garbage I saw was like millions of crayon marks
   on paper.

It looks like the fire crackers of the world being shot
    off,
But the best thing was it looked like itself—ugly, but
    nice in a way.

Andrew Vecchione

It
was
just
a
big
fat
old
hunk
junk
but
I
like
it
cause
he
was
my
brother

Jorge Robles

Behind the door
    there is a person
    with eyes of
    blue that shine

like a mirror
when it's clean
Behind the door
there is a
girl who is
I'd better
not tell you.

Ileana Mesen

On The Other Side of the Window

On the other
Side of the
Window in
School lies
The playground
And how I long
To be on the
Other side
Of the
Window

Tommy Kennedy

Along my house
I see a broken vase
In which the shiny
Colors green, yellow and
Blue shine in my eyes.

Hector Figueroa

Chapter Eight

FEDERICO GARCÍA LORCA

Romance Sonambulo

Verde que te quiero verde.
Verde viento. Verdes ramas.
El barco sobre la mar
y el caballo en la montaña.
Con la sombra en la cintura
ella sueña en su baranda,
verde carne, pelo verde,
con ojos de fría plata.
Verde que te quiero verde.
Bajo la luna gitana,
las cosas la están mirando
y ella no puede mirarlas.

Verde que te quiero verde.
Grandes estrellas de escarcha
vienen con el pez de sombra
que abre el camino del alba.
La higuera frota su viento
con la lija de sus ramas,
y el monte, gato garduño,
eriza sus pitas agrias.
¿Pero quién vendra? ¿Y por dónde . . .?
Ella sigue en su baranda,
verde carne, pelo verde,
soñando en la mar amarga.

—Compadre, quiero cambiar
mi caballo por su casa,
mi montura por su espejo,

mi cuchillo por su manta.
Compadre, vengo sangrando,
desde los puertos de Cabra.
—Si yo pudiera, mocito,
este trato se cerraba.
Pero yo ya no soy yo,
ni mi casa es ya mi casa.
—Compadre, quiero morir
decentemente en mi cama.
De acero, si puede ser,
con las sábanas de holanda.
¿No ves la herida que tengo
desde el pecho a la garganta?
—Trescientas rosas morenas
lleva tu pechera blanca.
Tu sangre rezuma y huele
alrededor de tu faja.
Pero yo ya no soy yo,
ni mi casa es ya mi casa.
—Dejadme subir al menos
hasta las altas barandas;
¡dejadme subir!, dejadme,
hasta las verdes barandas.
Barandales de la luna
por donde retumba el agua.
Ya suben los dos compadres
hacia las altas barandas.
Dejando un rastro de sangre.
Dejando un rastro de lágrimas.
Temblaban en los tejados
farolillos de hojalata.
Mil panderos de cristal
herían la madrugada.

Verde que te quiero verde,
verde viento, verdes ramas.
Los dos compadres subieron.
El largo viento dejaba
en la boca un raro gusto
de hiel, de menta y de albahaca.
¡Compadre! ¿Dónde está, díme?
¿Dónde está tu niña amarga?
¡Cuántas veces te esperó!
¡Cuántas veces te esperara,
cara fresca, negro pelo,
en esta verde baranda!

Sobre el rostro del aljibe
se mecía la gitana.
Verde carne, pelo verde,
con ojos de fría plata.
Un carámbano de luna
la sostiene sobre el agua.
La noche se puso íntima
como una pequeña plaza.
Guardias civiles borrachos
en la puerta golpeaban.
Verde que te quiero verde.
Verde viento. Verdes ramas.
El barco sobre la mar.
Y el caballo en la montaña.

Sleepwalking Ballad

Green, how I want you green.
Green wind. Green branches.
The ship out on the sea

and the horse on the mountain.
With the shade around her waist
she dreams on her balcony,
green flesh, her hair green,
with eyes of cold silver.
Green, how I want you green.
Under the gypsy moon,
all things are watching her
and she cannot see them.

Green, how I want you green.
Big hoarfrost stars
come with the fish of shadow
that opens the road of dawn.
The fig tree rubs its wind
with the sandpaper of its branches,
and the forest, cunning cat,
bristles its brittle fibers.
But who will come? And from where?
She is still on her balcony
green flesh, her hair green,
dreaming in the bitter sea.

—My friend, I want to trade
my horse for her house,
my saddle for her mirror,
my knife for her blanket.
My friend, I come bleeding
from the gates of Cabra.
—If it were possible, my boy,
I'd help you fix that trade.
But now I am not I,
nor is my house now my house.
—My friend, I want to die

decently in my bed.
Of iron, if that's possible,
with blankets of fine chambray.
Don't you see the wound I have
from my chest up to my throat?
—Your white shirt has grown
thirty dark brown roses.
Your blood oozes and flees
around the corners of your sash.
But now I am not I,
nor is my house now my house.
—Let me climb up, at least,
up to the high balconies;
Let me climb up! Let me,
up to the green balconies.
Railings of the moon
through which the water rumbles.

Now the two friends climb up,
up to the high balconies.
Leaving a trail of blood.
Leaving a trail of teardrops.
Tin bell vines
were trembling on the roofs.
A thousand crystal tambourines
struck at the dawn light.

Green, how I want you green,
green wind, green branches.
The two friends climbed up.
The stiff wind left
in their mouths, a strange taste
of bile, of mint, and of basil.
My friend, where is she— tell me—

where is your bitter girl?
How many times she waited for you!
How many times would she wait for you,
cool face, black hair,
on this green balcony!
Over the mouth of the cistern
the gypsy girl was swinging,
green flesh, her hair green,
with eyes of cold silver.
An icicle of moon
holds her up above the water.
The night became intimate
like a little plaza.
Drunken "Guardias Civiles"
were pounding on the door.
Green, how I want you green.
Green wind. Green branches.
The ship out on the sea.
And the horse on the mountain.

—*translated by William Logan*

Arbole, Arbole . . .

Arbolé, arbolé,
seco y verdé.

La niña del bello rostro
está cogiendo aceituna.
El viento, galán de torres,
la prende por la cintura.
Pasaron cuatro jinetes
sobre jacas andaluzas,

con trajes de azul y verde,
con largas capas oscuras.
"Vente a Córdoba, muchacha."
La niña no los esucha.
Pasaron tres torerillos
delgaditos de cintura,
con trajes color naranja
y espadas de plata antigua.
"Vente a Córdoba, muchacha."
La niña no los escucha.
Cuando la tarde se puso
morada, con lux difusa,
pasó un joven que llevaba
rosas y mirtos de luna.
"Vente a Granada, muchacha."
Y la niña no lo escucha.
La niña del bello rostro
sigue cogiendo aceituna,
con el brazo gris del viento
ceñido por la cintura.
Arbolé, arbolé.
Seco y verdé.

Arbole, Arbole . . .

Tree, tree
dry and green.

The girl with the pretty face
is out picking olives.
The wind, playboy of towers,
grabs her around the waist.
Four riders passed by

on Andalusian ponies,
with blue and green jackets
and big, dark capes.
"Come to Cordoba, muchacha."
The girl won't listen to them.
Three young bullfighters passed,
slender in the waist,
with jackets the color of oranges
and swords of ancient silver.
"Come to Sevilla, muchacha."
The girl won't listen to them.
When the afternoon had turned
dark brown, with scattered light,
a young man passed by, wearing
roses and myrtle of the moon.
"Come to Granada, muchacha."
And the girl won't listen to him.
The girl with the pretty face
keeps on picking olives
with the grey arm of the wind
wrapped around her waist.

Tree, tree
dry and green.

—translated by William Logan

FEDERICO GARCÍA LORCA

(SPANISH, 1898–1936)

Arbole, Arbole and *Romance Sonambulo*

I chose these poems because I felt their dreamy use of colors and their sense of magic places would appeal to children. I was drawn to the poems, too, because they are in Spanish, which gave me a chance to give my Spanish-speaking students some poetry in their language, and to heighten all my students' sense of the sound and color of words by having them compare, as they read, Spanish words with their English equivalents, and, when they wrote, having them use words in both languages. I think, before this, that many of the children hadn't ever really seen any poetry in another language. It was good to show them that there was such a thing, and to give them some idea of what a translation is.

I read the poems aloud, in English first; then as I went through the poems ("Arbole, Arbole" and the first 24 lines of "Romance Sonambulo," which seemed too long to go over in its entirety in class) along with explaining what was happening, I stopped at certain words or phrases to read them in Spanish as well as in English. I had the children close their eyes and listen, for example, to *"verde"* and "green" to *"verdes ramas"* and "green branches." I asked, "Which is greener? Which makes you see the most leaves?" I did the same with "moon" and *"luna,"* asking "Which is moonier? which is yellower? which more silvery?" The children answered enthusiastically, and by the time we had finished, they were excited about the sound of Spanish and English words. They were in a state to be thinking whether the sky outside the window was more blue or more *azul,* whether Aicza's dress was more orange or more *naranja,* whether, in fact, they'd prefer to be boys and girls or *niños* and *niñas.*

The poetry idea was, "Write a poem about a beautiful, strange place which is full of colors. Include some Spanish words in the poem. These may be color words, or any other words you find in the Lorca poems that you would like to use because of what they mean or just because you like the way

they look or sound—you don't have to know what they mean."
It may help the children with form to tell them that they can,
if they wish, put at least one color and one Spanish word in
every line; or that they can put one Spanish word for a color
(like *verde, plata,* or *naranja)* in every line. Some Spanish-
speaking students asked if they could write their whole poems
in Spanish, and Yuk asked me if instead of Spanish she could
use Chinese. I agreed to both requests. Yuk wrote her poem out
line by line in English, too; and when the all-Spanish poems
were completed I had their authors translate them into English.

The excitement and good feeling a lesson like this creates in
a class where many students know another language is something to see. There was a buzz as the Spanish-speaking students read over the Lorca poems, recognizing words and trying them out aloud; during the writing of the poems there was
constant interchange between those children who knew Spanish and those who didn't, those who didn't asking for the
meaning or pronunciation of words in the Lorca poems and
also for Spanish words to fit an English meaning they had in
mind. The Spanish-speaking children were very excited, too,
about translating their poems—flipping their paper over, they
got right to work and wrote quickly, obviously enjoying the
minor magic of translation. They also especially enjoyed reading the Spanish works aloud.

Even when children don't know the language, a foreign-
language poem accompanied by a translation can make for a
good class, because of the inspiration and excitement brought
on by the sight and sound of the strange and beautiful words.
I'd suggest, in fact, one class like this in any series of lessons.

My students created some fine vivid places, such as Lynne's
Rainy Storm Palace and Antoinette's palace with a "window
made of diamantes," Chip's completely blue (azul) world, Aicza's "planeta . . . de muchas colores," Mayra's green Mars,
Andrew's world under green mist. Some color images were
sharp and beautiful in the way Lorca's are, like Benny's "azul
water with verde boats and azul people" and Rebecca's ducks
on the lake next to a yellow flower. A few poems, Chip's and
Damary's, picked up Lorca's theme of desire for a color.

I didn't say much about the ballad aspects—story and characters—of "Romance Sonambulo," but a good lesson could be made by concentrating on those, too. The children could be asked to write a story poem, in which something dramatic happens, and to set the story in a strange place with many colors, and perhaps to give the characters and places Spanish names, using other Spanish words too if they wished. If the children like story poems, they might enjoy old English ballads, too, such as "Lord Randal" and "The Demon Lover."

The poems in this section using French words were written by French- and English-speaking students at the Newman School in New Orleans. Some of the ninth-grade Swaziland poems at the end of the book may also be of interest to children in connection with this lesson. The Swazi children learn English in school, but the language they speak at home is siSwati. Their poetry idea was to write a poem in English in which the name of at least one color in siSwati—such as *hlophe,* white; *luhlata,* green; *bomvu,* red—appears in every line. The mixture resulted in some strange and surprising lines which might help inspire children writing poems in any two languages.

FIFTH GRADE

Rojo rojo
Que bonito caballo
Cuando miro al caballo rojo
Me da gana de llorar
Porque rojo rojo ês un color maravilloso.

Red, red
What a pretty horse
When I look at my horse I feel
Like crying because red is a wonderful color.

Que bonito gatito
Cuando lo miro yo me da gracia
Porque el gatito es lindo.

What a pretty cat
When I look at him he makes me laugh
Because my cat is pretty.

Jennie Ortiz

Yo ví a una planeta y era de muchos colores y
los colores eran blanco y verde. Era bien bonitos.
Que lindos lindas eran los colores esos! A mi me
pasó una cosa. Me desnudé y me poni unas ropas
de plata. Después me empecé a despertar. Otra
vez me alegró a ver me mamá y mis amigos y
amigas y papa y hermanos y hermanas a mis
pies.

I went to a planet and it was of lots of colors.
They were white and green. They were very
pretty. What pretty, pretty colors. Something
happened to me. I took off my clothes and put on
clothes made out of silver. I woke up. I was
happy because I saw my mother, father, sisters,
brothers, and friends.

Aicza Bermudez

The color yellow is like the sun.
El color amarillo es como el sol.

The color red makes me happy.
El color rojo me hace feliz.

The color green makes me feel good.
El color verde me hace buena.

Carmen Berrios

if the city was verde
and the sea was verde
and things were verde think how Miss Pitts would
    look in verde
and the sky was verde and a little rojo in the ground
Verde verde verde. I wish the sea was verde
The sea is verde are you verde.

Damary Hernandez

Verde looks like the water at night—azul water with verde boats and azul people.

Benny Vincifora

Blue is the ocean
Nice is the sky
Huge are the buildings

Azul es el mar.
Lindo es el celo.
Que casas mas lindas y grandes

Jose Castillo

Azul

   Oh azul oh azul everything is azul from the tip
of its tail to top of its nose it's azul everything it
is azul but alas it turns Verde for the day's night
but in the morning it will be azul again and I will
come, it will be azul from the tip of its tail to top
of its nose, yes It will be azul.

                                    Chip Wareing

Poem

At six o'clock the buildings seemed rojo.
At twelve o'clock the sky turned a beautiful azul.
It was time to dress up in verde.
My bet was lost because clay turned rojo.
And the sun became as yellow as a montaña de plata.
The blackboard is turning as blanco as his Sunday
        shirt.

                        Kenneth Koch and Rosa Rosario

Red,   yellow,   white, black,   brown,   pink.

紅, 黃, 白, 黑, 棕, 粉紅.

Green   restaurant.

綠 飯 店.

Big   red   sun.

大 紅 太 陽

Yuk Leung

El Sueño de la Flor Amarilla—
The Dream of the Yellow Flower

Cuando el sol brilla la flor tiene mas alum-
bración si no tene agua la flor se muere los pati-
tos nadan en el charco de agua se ven muy lindos
alado de una flor amarilla.

When the sun brights the flower has
    brightness. If it doesn't have water it
    would die.

The ducks swim in a lake of water it looks so
    pretty next to a yellow flower.

Rebecca Crespo

Once when I went home it was boring so I went to a
building that was being rebuilt
And I built myself a palace named after the beautiful
queen Miss Pitts (she was an old devil with horns
but I wanted to make her happy) herself with a
verde baranda
And a plata montaña with walls of plata and oro
And a window made of diamantes and I had dresses
made of the finest soies in the land.
And all my friends would come and see me the
queen.

Antoinette Anderson

The City of Adventure

One day in the City of Verde there was a terrible fall of ramas. The gitana crashed into the
earth. All of the people ran to the plata house
where they were protected. There were no heat-
ers in the plata house so the people died of escarcha.

Steven Lenik

In Rainy Storm Palace the estrellas are a pretty color of verde, the luna is a pretty color of plata. The color of the people is amarillo, and the montañas are very high y punta. Also the amarge is a pretty color of azul.

Lynne Reif

Los hombres son el color verde y las mujers son el color amarillo y los muchachos son el color verde y amarillo.

The men are the color green and the ladies are the color yellow and the children are the color green and yellow.

Wilson Perez

Los Colores

La noche es negra como la oscuridad del mar. El cielo es azul como el cielo.

Carmen Aponte

SIXTH GRADE

Mars the Green Green Planet

Green wind. Green branches
Everything you see is green
Green snowflakes, green green songs
Will sing upn the green green hill.
Mañana tomorrow everything will turn azul and
    amarillo like the blue azul sky.
I must go now.
Soon the green fades away and everything will
    vanish.

Mayra Morales

The World Under Green Mist

Under the moon's green mist lie dreams of beauty
    and wonder
There are beds of fur from a fox
The warmth of the fireplace glows sparks of wonder
With the peaceful dark of the night lie fire bugs
    flickering their lights
Oh under this world with green mist lie the dreams
    of every person
Hidden from them until they die.

Andrew Vecchione

As I Sailed

The sea was amarillo
with waves of rojo
The sun azul
And the sky gris
This was all this
As I sailed
In my verde boat.

Sedley Alpaugh

A verde mushroom
With a morado stem
Started to turn rojo
In the amarillo sun.

Sedley Alpaugh

I have a Persuvius
The only one on the block
His legs are wine color
Rouge with violet spots
His verte colored neck
Flashes in the noir sun
He flows along the ground in a blanc stream.

Author unknown

By the azul lake and the azure sky,
A small morado poppy stood
With a blanco dewdrop on its head.
The waves rippled and the verde grass rippled

While the morado poppy swayed back and forth.
The waves hit the café ground
And covered the poppy and the verde grass,
Burying and killing them both.

Melanie Myers

La grenouille est verte
Pourquoi?
Le coq est orange
Pourquoi?
Le lapin est brun
Pourquoi?
Pourquoi je suis une couleur?

Stephen Godchaux

The Thing

In a way the thing was morado,
But yet there was a touch of azul shining here and
    there
It seemed as though I saw a sliver of amarillo
    shining
Like a diamond in a negro night
The rojo color in it, was as rojo as a sports car and
Still as blanco as a naranja sky.

Susan Strug

Chapter Nine

JOHN ASHBERY

Into the Dusk-Charged Air

Far from the Rappahannock, the silent
Danube moves along toward the sea.
The brown and green Nile rolls slowly
Like the Niagara's welling descent.
Tractors stood on the green banks of the Loire
Near where it joined the Cher.
The St. Lawrence prods among black stones
And mud. But the Arno is all stones.
Wind ruffles the Hudson's
Surface. The Irawaddy is overflowing.
But the yellowish, gray Tiber
Is contained within steep banks. The Isar
Flows too fast to swim in, the Jordan's water
Courses over the flat land. The Allegheny and its
    boats
Were dark blue. The Moskowa is
Gray boats. The Amstel flows slowly.
Leaves fall into the Connecticut as it passes
Underneath. The Liffey is full of sewage,
Like the Seine, but unlike
The brownish-yellow Dordogne.
Mountains hem in the Colorado
And the Oder is very deep, almost
As deep as the Congo is wide.
The plain banks of the Neva are
Gray. The dark Saône flows silently.
And the Volga is long and wide
As it flows across the brownish land. The Ebro
Is blue, and slow. The Shannon flows

Swiftly between its banks. The Mississippi
Is one of the world's longest rivers, like the Amazon.
It has the Missouri for a tributary.
The Harlem flows amid factories
And buildings. The Nelson is in Canada,
Flowing. Through hard banks the Dubawnt
Forces its way. People walk near the Trent.
The landscape around the Mohawk stretches away;
The Rubicon is merely a brook.
In winter the Main
Surges; the Rhine sings its eternal song.
The Rhône slogs along through whitish banks
And the Rio Grande spins tales of the past.
The Loire bursts its frozen shackles
But the Moldau's wet mud ensnares it.
The East catches the light.
Near the Escaut the noise of factories echoes
And the sinuous Humboldt gurgles wildly.
The Po too flows, and the many-colored
Thames. Into the Atlantic Ocean
Pours the Garonne. Few ships navigate
On the Housatonic, but quite a few can be seen
On the Elbe. For centuries
The Afton has flowed.

                    If the Rio Negro
Could abandon its song, and the Magdalena
The jungle flowers, the Tagus
Would still flow serenely, and the Ohio
Abrade its slate banks. The tan Euphrates would
Sidle silently across the world. The Yukon
Was choked with ice, but the Susquehanna still
        pushed
Bravely along. The Dee caught the day's last flares

Like the Pilcomayo's carrion rose.
The Peace offered eternal fragrance
Perhaps, but the Mackenzie churned livid mud
Like tan chalk-marks. Near where
The Brahmaputra slapped swollen dikes
Was an opening through which the Limmat
Could have trickled. A young man strode the
    Churchill's
Banks, thinking of night. The Vistula seized
The shadows. The Theiss, stark mad, bubbled
In the windy evening. And the Ob shuffled
Crazily along. Fat billows encrusted the Dniester's
Pallid flood, and the Fraser's porous surface.
Fish gasped amid the Spree's reeds. A boat
Descended the bobbing Orinoco. When the
Marne flowed by the plants nodded
And above the glistering Gila
A sunset as beautiful as the Athabaska
Stammered. The Zambezi chimed. The Oxus
Flowed somewhere. The Parnahyba
Is flowing, like the wind-washed Cumberland.
The Araguayo flows in the rain.
And, through overlying rocks the Isère
Cascades gently. The Guadalquivir sputtered.
Someday time will confound the Indre,
Making a rill of the Hwang. And
The Potomac rumbles softly. Crested birds
Watch the Ucalyali go
Through dreaming night. You cannot stop
The Yenisei. And afterwards
The White flows strongly to its . . .
Goal. If the Tyne's shores
Hold you, and the Albany
Arrest your development, can you resist the Red's

Musk, the Meuse's situation?
A particle of mud in the Neckar
Does not turn it black. You cannot
Like the Saskatchewan, nor refuse
The meandering Yangtze, unleash
The Genesee. Does the Scamander
Still irrigate crimson plains? And the Durance
And the Pechora? The São Francisco
Skulks amid gray, rubbery nettles. The Liard's
Reflexes are slow, and the Arkansas erodes
Anthracite hummocks. The Paranya stinks.
The Ottawa is light emerald green
Among grays. Better that the Indus fade
In steaming sands! Let the Brazos
Freeze solid! And the Wabash turn to a leaden
Cinder of ice! The Marañon is too tepid, we must
Find a way to freeze it hard. The Ural
Is freezing slowly in the blasts. The black Yonne
Congeals nicely. And the Petit-Morin
Curls up on the solid earth. The Inn
Does not remember better times, and the
    Merrimack's
Galvanized. The Ganges is liquid snow by now;
The Vyatka's ice-gray. The once-molten Tennessee's
Curdled. The Yapura is a pack of ice. Gelid
The Columbia's gray loam banks. The Don's merely
A giant icicle. The Niger freezes, slowly.
The interminable Lena plods on
But the Purus' mercurial waters are icy, grim
With cold. The Loing is choked with fragments of ice.
The Weser is frozen, like liquid air.
And so is the Kama. And the beige, thickly flowing
Tocantins. The rivers bask in the cold.
The stern Uruguay chafes its banks,

A mass of ice. The Hong-Chu is solid
Ice. The Adour is silent, motionless.
The lovely Tigris is nothing but scratchy ice
Like the Yellowstone, with its osier-clustered banks.
The Mekong is beginning to thaw out a little
And the Donets gurgles beneath the
Huge blocks of ice. The Manzanares gushes free.
The Illinois darts through the sunny air again.
But the Dnieper is still ice-bound. Somewhere
The Salado propels its floes, but the Roosevelt's
Frozen. The Oka is frozen solider
Than the Somme. The Minho slumbers
In winter, nor does the Snake
Remember August. Hilarious, the Canadian
Is solid ice. The Madeira slavers
Across the thawing fields, and the Plata laughs.
The Dvina soaks up the snow. The Sava's
Temperature is above freezing. The Avon
Carols noiselessly. The Drôme presses
Grass banks; the Adige's frozen
Surface is like gray pebbles.

Birds circle the Ticino. In winter
The Var was dark blue, unfrozen. The
Thwaite, cold, is choked with sandy ice;
The Ardèche glistens feebly through the freezing
    rain.

JOHN ASHBERY

(AMERICAN, 1927–   )

Into the Dusk-Charged Air

I thought this poem would appeal to children for its lovely convincing river descriptions and for its way of seeming, as it goes along, like a geography book gone mad—there are a hundred and fifty rivers in it, with a little comment about each. The poem stirs up a pleasant "How many can you name" feeling, which makes children eager to write.

I began the class by asking for the names of rivers. The children had big geography books of Africa on their desks, so I asked for some names of rivers from there. I wrote them on the board: the Congo, the Nile, the Niger, and so on. Then I asked for rivers from all over: the Mississippi, the Ohio, the Seine, the Tiber. After I had a long list on the board, I asked the children questions: What color is the Delaware? "Yellow." What kind of sound does it make? "A soft sound." "A loud sound." "A yellow sound." What time of year is the Niger like? "Fall."

The poetry idea was, "Write a poem with a different river in each line." I tried to get the children to really have feelings about each river. I said, "Try to think what color the river is, what sort of sound it makes, what time of year it makes you think of. Think what it would be like to be really on each river, in its country floating down it in a boat, or swimming in it, looking at the shore, seeing trees, buildings, animals. Just think about everything you can about each river to make it really seem to be rushing through your poem. Is it a cold river? warm? Are there birds over it? Are there any other people on it? What does the sky look like when you're floating on it?" After all this, and after soliciting some sample lines from the children, I read the first twenty-five lines of Ashbery's poem aloud to them. In most other lessons I began with the adult poem, but here I brought it into the lesson after they were already excited about the subject. I said about the poem, "This, essentially, is the kind of thing I want you all to do in your poems." Then I had them write.

The children wrote a great variety of fine poems about serious rivers, "silly rivers" (to use Fontessa's phrase), romantic rivers, and polluted rivers. Many of their lines seem to have caught some of the sophistication, complexity, and humor of Ashbery's listing of rivers, such as Ilona's about the Amazon and the Yangtze, Tommy Kennedy's about the Hudson and the Delaware, Eliza's about the Congo, the Thames, and the East. Others, like Stephen's and Guy's, were more personal, lyrical, and dreamlike. All the poems showed the children's pleasure in being able to use a serious school subject, geography, in an imaginative and free-wheeling way.

The Ashbery class came before I had begun teaching adult poetry in a systematic fashion. Like the class in which I used D. H. Lawrence's "The White Horse," it was one that showed me it could be done. The order of events, giving the children the poem so late in the class, in this case worked out well, and I think it might, too, with other big simple list kinds of poems in which the main appeal is the dazzle and variety of many individual instances. Some of Whitman's great lists in "Song of Myself" might be taught this way, for example. With such poems, the children may be more inspired by exercising their own ingenuity and imagination first, then being given, rather quickly, some splendid examples to stir their emulative feelings and to quicken some of the ideas they already have. If possible, of course, the children should also have copies of the poem to read afterward and take home with them.

FIFTH GRADE

Rivers

The Rhine River is red paint rushing down the rocks
    in Russia.
I see myself in a raft on the Don River hitting the
    rocks coming downstream.

There I can see below the top rocks the soft silent
water swaying back and forth against the rocks.
The Yukon River with its light blue water rushes and
roughs its water in the day and softens in the
evening.
I can see the Amazon River with its violet water
brushing at my face and it feels so cool and
creamy like I could stay there forever.
The Yangtze River is yellow with pretty glowing
white rocks in the early morning and the empty
bridge is strong and healthy.

Ilona Baburka

Rivers of the World

The Delaware River is like the color blue with people
falling in.
The Mississippi River is like July and people
jumping out of the window.
The Nile River is like being in an airplane in the
rain.
The East River is like air pollution in May is black
all around.
The Colorado River is like the color blue with people
drowning.
The Harlem River is like the color black and it is like
July in the snow.
The Congo River is like purple in August in the rain
and snow.

Rodney Wills

The black shadows of the Rhine shine on Germany.
The green waters of the Shannon shine on Ireland.
The rusty waters of the East River shine on the black
    sidewalks of the Battery Manhattan.
The orange waters of the Orange River shine on
    Africa.
And the sailing waters of the Hudson shine on the
    town of Poughkeepsie and the train tracks on its
    bank.
The Delaware River still has George Washington's
    wiggly line of his boat going across.

Tommy Kennedy

What Rivers Make Me Think Of

The Colorado makes me think about red apples
    because it sounds like the color red in Spanish.
The river Congo makes me think about the color
    white because it sounds like the name of coconut
    in Spanish.
The river Yangtze makes me think of a baseball team
    because it sounds like the name of a baseball
    team called the Yankees.
The Nile River makes me think of a file because they
    both rhyme.
The Arno River makes me think of the name of a boy
    in my class called Arnaldo.
And the last river makes me think of lots of things.

Jose Lopez

Rivers

The Mississippi River is like the nice light blue of a
   nice sunny day in June.
The Nile River is like when you have just done
   something wonderful and they thank you for it.
The Yellow River is like when you have just come
   from the beach.
The rivers are like the soft green grass in a nice park
   or forest.
You just can't imagine how nice a river can be. But
   when you think of rivers you think of the
   wonderful things in the world.
But if all the pollution keeps on we will not have any
   rivers to think of and enjoy looking at.

Vilma Mejias

*What Would Happen if All the Rivers and Seas and
Lakes in the World Were Attached Together*

Once I was walking along the shore and all of
a sudden the Red Sea was getting real red and it
started to grow. Like a magnet it pulled the
Orange and Yellow Sea. It looked like a rainbow.
Then came the Darling River walking hand in
hand with Lake Victoria and the Mississippi
River. They all wore blue and green. It looked
like they were dancing on the rainbow of seas as
they chatted and gossiped as women usually do.
Then came the Shannon catching up with the

women. Then came the Nile turned Nile Delta.
They all rush on the rainbow of seas making a
quiet shiny sound as night came upon them.
That was only part of the rivers. Other parts of
the world saw the rest. But they never saw the
rainbow rivers with the ballroom of dancing
lakes and oceans as night fell and all of it disap-
pears. Come back again and visit me, my quiet
little friends.

Marion Mackles

Rivers and My Mind

I'm going in the dark gray waters of the Amazon
Within those dark gray waters I see
I see the most beautiful fish ever seen
I head into the Delta Nile River and still swim
    onward
I'm beginning to go into the Niger River.
       This is my last stop

        Auf wieder sehn.

Stephen Sebbane

Serious Rivers

I don't like to go swimming in the green East River.
I love to go ice skating on the Martian River on Mars.
I like to see and go on old boats on the yellow Hong
  Kong River.

I saw Mr. Kenneth Koch in a brown suit on Lake
    Victoria.
I like to go on a gondola on the canals of Venice.
I like to take movies of the Amazon River of a green
    lizard jumping up and down going clippity clop.
I like to see a white goat with a sign saying "Buy the
    new book Wishes, Lies, and Dreams by Kenneth
    Koch and tell him Thomas Rogasky age 10½ sent
    you" on the Yukon River.

                                    Thomas Rogasky

Beautiful Rivers

The Orange River with the yellow sunshine shining
    down.
The East River so full of pollution.
The Nile Delta in a little rowboat eating watermelon.
The Rhine with the sea gulls above and the moon
    glowing in the dark.
The Congo the drums playing.
The Hong Kong the sea flowing past me.
The Tanga in the middle of the sea on a little boat
    with my dog Tammy.
The Yellow River the blaze of the wind.
The East River in a boat dragons coming out of the
    water.
The Amazon and I look up to the sky and the stars
    are horoscope signs.
Look I found mine.

                                    Vivien Tuft

Rivers

I am sailing down the blue Nile and I hear a pin
    dropping.
I am sailing on the Mississippi's yellow waters and I
    hear a fire crackling on shore on July Fourth.
I am rowing down the Nile while I hear a Chinese
    person singing in February.
I am sailing down the Delta on my new sailboat
    while I hear a fish in the water on April First.
I am rowing down the Niger on a red morning while
    I hear African people talking.

Billy Constant

I dived into the Nile River and came out blue
and I was wearing a blue Yangtze River. Then I
started to melt in the different rivers and colors
and wishes, I was a river of dreams. It happened.
I melted once more and turned into a river of
dreams. People drank me and became happy
again. Some people would put me in a glass and
look at me, dream about happy things, and then
drink me and go everywhere. Then I sneezed
and I was back in school writing this poem.

Guy Peters

Rivers

The Nile flows past gently carrying boats
As the Missouri flows roughly past houses it invites
    children to swim
The wind sweeps over the Hudson ever so hard
As the Congo River runs swiftly it draws women
    from the houses to wash their clothes
The Thames River runs along as swiftly as a country
    brook
As the East River runs the pollution hangs over it
    like a threatening cloud

Eliza Bailey

The Silly Rivers—The City of Rivers

One day in Paris I was walking by the river
And the river began to say, "Little girl, what is your
    name?"
I simply replied, "My name is Fontessa."
The river said, "My name is Mr. Koch."
Then I walked away, then I came to another river
And it said the same thing as the first.
That river's name was Miss Pitts the Great.
Then I came to another river, and its name
Was Allen and his mermaid Joanne.
Then I came to another river, and his name
Was Bernie the Moustache River,
Which made me laugh.

Then I came to another river
And its name was Eric the Skinny Bone.
Then I kept on walking to a little river
And its name was Hector the Idiot.
Then I walked on to my little house
And there I dreamed about the rivers I passed!!!
Which were very sweet rivers except Hector the
    Idiot!!!!

Fontessa Moore

My Rivers

If I were sitting near the Delaware I would wave
    hello to George Washington
If I were sitting near the Shannon I would put my
    feet in her cool water and she would pinch me
If I were sitting near Rhine we'd get together and try
    to think up a new name for her.
If I were sitting next to the Orange river I would give
    her a starkist orange
If I were sitting next to the Danube river I'd sprinkle
    a blanket of stars over her.
And then I'd put the Don and Volga together to make
    some more *Rivers*

Tracy Lahab

Rivers of Different Signs

Delaware—green with April birds and flowers
Missouri—red January bugs and laughter
Amazon—yellow, August beauty and ugliness
Mississippi—river of orange leaves and trees of
    autumn
Hudson—apples of red March of butterflies and
    balloons and chipmunks chirping
East River—river of children playing with blue
    swimsuits with blue polkadots
Harlem—river with frogs and blue-red butterflies
Yangtze—river of yellow watermelons waiting to be
    eaten in the warm April weather
Darling—river of beauty and kindness helping
    children walk the line of happiness
Nile Delta—last river I'll ever see.

Mayra Morales

Chapter Ten

ARTHUR RIMBAUD

Voyelles

A noir, E blanc, I rouge, U vert, O bleu: voyelles,
Je dirai quelque jour vos naissances latentes:
A, noir corset velu des mouches éclatantes
Qui bombinent autour des puanteurs cruelles,

Golfes d'ombre; E, candeurs des vapeurs et des tentes,
Lances des glaciers fiers, rois blancs, frissons
    d'ombelles;
I, pourpres, sang craché, rire des lèvres belles
Dans la colère ou les ivresses pénitentes;

U, cycles, vibrements divins des mers virides,
Paix des pâtis semés d'animaux, paix des rides
Que l'alchimie imprime aux grands fronts studieux;

O, suprême Clairon plein de strideurs étranges,
Silences traversés des Mondes et des Anges:
—O l'Oméga, rayon violet de Ses Yeux!

Vowels

Black A, white E, red I, green U, blue O—vowels,
I'll tell, some day, your secret origins:
A, black hairy corset of dazzling flies
Who boom around cruel stenches,

Gulfs of darkness; E, candor of steam and of tents,
Lances of proud glaciers, white kings, Queen-
    Anne's-lace shivers;
I, deep reds, spit blood, laughter of beautiful lips
In anger or in drunkenness and penitence;

U, cycles, divine vibrations of dark green oceans,
Peacefulness of pastures dotted with animals, the
    peace of wrinkles
Which alchemy prints on studious foreheads;

O, supreme trumpet, full of strange harsh sounds,
Silences which are crossed by Worlds and by Angels—
    O, Omega, violet ray of Her Eyes!

—translated by Kenneth Koch

Voyelles

From the time I started teaching poetry to children I had thought of teaching them "Voyelles." Rimbaud's poem, written when he was only sixteen, with its sensuous association of colors and vowels is, whatever else it is, a magical childlike kind of game. The poem has the charm of a crazy but serious alphabet book, which teaches you not something practical but something mysterious. Anyone who has ever used crayons or colored chalk or read an alphabet book has associations of letters with colors, and I knew from my children's earlier work that they naturally associated colors with sounds as well ("A rose is as red as a beating of drums . . . /The tree is as green as a roaring lion. . . .").

When I was asked to teach a class at the Lycée Français in New York last spring, it seemed like a good occasion to try teaching "Voyelles." My students at the Lycée were ninth- and tenth-graders who knew both English and French. I taught the poem just as I would have taught it at PS 61—discussing it, making it dramatic, giving a poetry idea, asking for sample lines, having them write, then read their poems aloud.

The poetry idea for "Voyelles" was, "Write a poem in which in every line you give the color of a vowel and also mention a few things which have that color. If you like, you can say that these things are the origin of the colors and of the vowels." Since the Lycée students knew French, I suggested they write about the vowels in both French and English. The most important things to tell students are, first, to really listen to the vowel and decide on a color for it; and, second, to be as free and surprising as Rimbaud is in choosing the things which have that color. He doesn't use any of the ordinary examples of whiteness, for instance, such as snow or lilies, but really surprising ones, which make you see something new: the whiteness of steam, the whiteness of tents, the shining white pointed projecting parts (like lances) of glaciers, white kings (chess pieces? or kings wrapped in ermine robes?), and the shivering of Queen-Anne's-lace.

To help the Lycée students associate colors with sounds, I did the same kind of thing I did in elementary school—asked them to close their eyes and listen while I pronounced vowels and to tell me what colors they sounded like. Their responses were somewhat more restrained that those of my younger students, but they were just as sensitive to the associations and as sure about their rightness. I asked for color associations with consonants, as well, and with numbers. After that I went through Rimbaud's poem and made sure they could see each of his color examples clearly. The more sharply they could actually visualize his glaciers, tents, and pastures dotted with animals, the more likely they were to create vivid visual experiences in their own poems. After asking the students to tell me some sample lines ("O is red, a postage stamp and an autumn moon. . . ."), I had everyone write one or two such lines quickly, and turn them in to me, after which I read some aloud. Then they wrote their longer poems.

Though I taught the Lycée students in the same way I taught younger children, their poems were different in significant ways. The quality of these poems, in keeping with these children's greater verbal abilities, seemed assurance that this way of teaching was as appropriate to high school as to elementary school. These students had vocabularies and general verbal abilities not to be found in elementary school, as well as a wide range of reference and some sophistication about poetry. Their poems mentioned Matisse, the Russian czar, traveling to Thailand, banshees, the waters of Venice, and the fiery gold curtains at Carnegie Hall. They were capable of such sophisticated phrasing as "Quick open breathing of a rock in seagulls' incandescent swoops" and "The Y is pink and begins with the delicate chit-chat of a silly darling creature." And they could come as close to Rimbaud's amazing richness and complexity as "Precious jewels strewn on coral reefs by soft mermaids." What the poetry of older and younger children had in common was vivacity and freshness, and excitement about words and about the chance to express secret feelings.

NINTH AND TENTH GRADES

I is green and started in a dark forest at dawn, it's
    Cleopatra's eyeshadow, a balloon you would buy
    at the zoo.
A is yellow, a very light yellow like the sun on a cold
    and clear morning, and the color of the vitamins
    I had to take when I was sick.
O is blue like the snow before night falls or the
    runway at the airport.
E is red, the deep red of a Spanish woman's lips, or E
    can be purple and it reminds me of death, of a
    funeral.
U can be grey the color of stones in the country, or
    the color of peasoup at camp, or the muddy color
    of the Mississippi.

Martine Nicolas

Parenthèses

Le U est orange, il se trouve sur l'eau au couchant.
The A is chocolate brown and one can always see it
    under the bark of a rotten branch on a pine tree.
Le E est bleu pâle, and sounds like a breathing cry.
I is tan, but green; snow in shadow on top of my
    mountain, where I found a moldy scarf.

Le O est bleu-vert comme l'eau, qui scintille en
   tombant éternellement sur les durs rochers froids.
E is white with the empty depth of black; hard sheets
   of ice, shining in the sun.

Mary L. Bowden

Moments

The U is red, the banshee's coat, the chair back's
   tacks
Le A est or, le manteau du messager et le chapeau de
   la script-girl.
Ou est vert-bleu, les eaux de Venise, la barbe, le sac
   sur la chaise et mes yeux.
Oy; grey
Blond hair blue, I, shoe buckles or.
Russian: half-way between red and green
The legs of the tables sound like green, green as E,
   green like the paperclips holding the sea to the
   land, the shore.

Peter Michael Basch

Nothing Much

O is green and is the cry of a clipper's figurehead as
   she battles a gale.
S black: the rich folds of a velvet gown rustling on a
   castle floor.
E is white as a pyramid in the glare of an Egyptian
   sun

A is blue & is my screech as a wave hits me, while
   I'm hiking out trying to flatten a boat (or as I fall
   off a trapeze).
P is pink as precise as the movements of a dancer's
   shoes.

Anne Lincoff

La Jeunesse

The A is blue like hate in a confused mind.
The I is silvery like a cruel word.
The E is black like captivity
The U is leaf-green like freedom
The O is white like purity.

Catherine Blanc

Le U est la lumière du phare dans une nuit nuagée;
   c'est le gris flottant, envelopant, des soirées
   paisibles à la campagne.
O is red with purple waves, vineyards undulating in
   the sunny wind, women with big hats and men
   with baggy trousers. A raised, burning red
   eyebrow. Fiery gold curtains raising at Carnegie.
U brown, from muddy pastures where legendary
   cows with soft pink noses look in vain for grass.
   The old flowered wallpaper in the empty rooms
   in the empty house on the marsh.
E couleur des mers tropiques. Precious jewels strewn
   on coral reefs by soft mermaids. Poissons
   pensants, rois fiers!

Jessica Levine

The Wilderness

A: Red, from
straight, red rivers,
rigid, slow not
thick nor watery, shallow
and constant, lukewarm,
with the smell of clay

E: blueish green, weak in
strength, distributed mixed together
(blue and green) unequally over a
plain, with disgust hidden within.

I: white, and gold,
as when an egg is broken open.

O: brown, from meadows of
vegetation deprived of water for a short amount
of
time, moved by the air, quiet and somber,
the sun going down.

U: orange-yellow, uniformly
mixed, with the taste
of Tang without the sweetness,
stingy, that you can move
your fingers through, but
which separates,
like mercury, into isolated gatherings

Author unknown

The Man on the Shore

C is the white gull flying above the mast
A est rouge comme le phare réconfortant
O is the green of the sea I saw in May
I is the color of the boat ou the river far ahead
B la couleur du bateau du pêcheur perdu dans la
    tempête
U the color of the wind passing through the broken
    masts
O la couleur des vagues qui viennent s'échouer sur le
    rivage
I c'est la brise qui souffle sur les visages anxieux

                            Philippe Géraud

Grey O braille whistle of wind on a ripped wall
Largo prayer of dusty lips
Quick open breathing of a rock in seagulls'
    incandescent swoops.
Highway zoom into Chinese clouds
Oboes oboes oboes.
O rose cil roses contre une fenêtre bronzée d'orgue
    frémissant de lumière

                          Gina Kovarsky

Inspiration Lost

Le a est gris, je l'ai cueilli sur la queue bouffante
    d'une jument verte.
The e is crackled yellow, I found it in my bath.
The y is orange, it was discovered by Matisse under
    the table.
Le y est violet, un czar russe l'a laissé tomber dans
    les profoundeurs de ma bouche.
Le i est jaune, il est sorti, joyeux, du coin de mon oeil.
Malgré ceci, I hate letters.

                        Nadejda Kondratiev

Les Rides de Couleur

Le U c'est le maure vêtu d'une lourde robe blanche,
    étendu sur un bloc de ciment mat entouré d'un
    désert de sable noir.
Un désert noir d'un éclat foudroyant qui noie
    l'univers entier dans la profondeur de ses antres.
Le A c'est la peur, la peur rougeoyante des roues du
    temps qui nous écrasent au fond d'un puits qui
    m' engloutit dans son eau de velours pourpre.
Le O c'est l'aboiement orange d'un chien. C'est
    l'exclamation hideuse des personnes flasques et
    molles. C'est l'opéra.
Le E c'est le bleu, couleur d'azur d'un monde infini.
    C'est l'espace entre la mer des sables et des
    océans grondants dans le pouvoir infini de ma
    main crispée.

                 Dimitri Moliavko-Visotzky

A.E.I.O.U.

Le A c'est une bouche ouverte, avec la langue qui
    pend,
Alouette est le 1er mot qui me surprend.

A is the air, it floats,
This is my life like a wandering boat.

E is everything, to me it is shiny lower teeth.
E c'est l'hôpital, plein de gens malades qui toussent.

I c'est une abeille, elle pique.
I is me.

O is the abyss a dark deep hole in the ground
O c'est de l'eau.

U c'est tu, vu, lu,
U is you your mouth shaped like an "O" while you
    are pronouncing this letter.

Stephen Samson

Nu

A écarlate, le caillou dégringole la pente et le volcan
    nait.
I or, the bird has flown away, try not to cry.
O noir, c'est froid et triste, tout seul sur cette chaise
E silvery, the air feels heavy a shriek from the
    corner, I wonder what happened.
U purple like the poet's sweater maybe gay sweet
    happy.
U gentil, on trébuche et tombe dans le ruisseau,
    bruyant splash.

Van-Thi Nguyen

Bleu de Douceur

Le E est né dans le bleu du ciel d'été
Dans une boîte de pastels
Ou la couverture du petit bébé
Et dans les yeux et les boucles d'oreille de Mme.
    Ingalls.

Ioana Giurgui

Different Feeling

Le O est noir, on l'a trouvé au fond de l'océan.
The O is dark silvery blue and it was found among
    all the planets.
E is yellow like a smile;
Le U is red like rubber on the sole of a shoe.

Le E est doux et rose.

Le I est jaune, peut-être orange comme un voyage en
Thailande.

Y est fort comme le métal, profond comme l'océan. Il
n'a pas de couleur.

Michèle Pouget

The "Y" is pink and begins with the delicate
chit-chat of a silly darling creature.

Le "A" est bleu pâle et jaune vif, il commence avec
"en garde" et finit avec "touché."

Chantal Clesca

The Indian

Le E est le bleu et se trouve dans la nuit noire des
sorciers hypocrites

E represents the shocking red of a kingly throne, the
red of the damned hell.

U est beige et vient du vol clair et lent de l'hirondelle
vantarde.

U is blue and comes from the transparent sheet of
music easing through the piano.

O est jaune et vient des châteaux-forteresses des
amoureux enfantins

O is white and comes from the pink tongue of the
nebulous sun.

A est le rouge de la pomme pourrie

A is orange and falls from the bottomless pit in the
    bullring
I est le brun sombre d'un long chapeau pointu
I is the colorless me who cries at the death of an
    imaginary wave.
P is the black crow upon a coin, fluttering his downy
    feathers upon a wish

Vivianne Hanania

Associations Fades

Le U est glauque, comme les rides glacées des
    fondrières
Dans lesquelles plongent les pieds d'un enfant
U is brown, sweat dripping off from a horse's back
Running wild in a flashing streak of filthy gold.
S, la fuite silencieuse d'un serpent traqué par son
    ombre,
Rampant, sali par la glue de son corps.
N, le son d'une pénombre
Floue, mystérieuse; les vagues d'une cloche
Qui s'évadent et se volatilisent dans une goutte
Moite, d'alcool camphré.
X, le fixe qui se propage dans l'éternité
D'un baiser
Et meurt inexorablement, flasque et faible, flasque et
    faible, flasque et faible

Gilles Beaulne

Mais Bonne en Sports

Le Y est jaune
Il est doux et tranquille
On ne le voit pas souvent;
C'est la jeune fille timide qui
Avait autrefois de longs cheveux
Jaunes et soyeux et qui
Se les fit couper pour
Qu'on ne l'aperçût pas trop souvent

Author unknown

Senses

Le A est rouge et il commence dans l'Enfer,
The A is red and it begins in an Apple.

Le A est jaune et il vient d'un poussin,
The A is yellow and it starts on a wall.

The O is blue-grey and it glides in the water,
Le O est noir-blanc et il vient de la bouche.

The E is black, and it stretches across the page.
Le E est noir et il s'arrête brusquement.

Le I est blanc, et chante à voix haute.
The I is brown, and is very steadfast.

Le U est lavande, et me semble bizarre.
The U is pink, and one can ride it.

The O is dark blue, and circles the moon.
Le O est gris, et ne me croit pas.

The I is pink and white, and it's cold and icy.
Le I est blanchâtre, et flotte jusqu'au ciel.

The E is black, and a spider on the crawl.
Le E est vert-olive, et me semble tout bête.

Diana Flescher

Anthology

Restricting children to poems supposed to be on their age-
or grade-level deprives them of too many good things. They
get more out of genuinely good poems than out of mediocre
ones, even if the better poems are difficult in some ways. The
aim of this anthology is to suggest a number of fine poems, in
addition to those discussed in the preceding chapters, that
children can enjoy reading and that teachers can enjoy teaching. Each poem is followed by a poetry idea and sometimes
also by a few other notes on teaching it. These are only suggestions, of course—particular class situations and a teacher's
feelings about particular poems may suggest changes or new
approaches altogether. Changes the children themselves may
propose for the poetry idea are usually very helpful in making
the idea more inspiring to them.

I chose the poems with third-through-sixth-grade students
in mind, children from eight to twelve years old. With the
younger children it might be good to begin with poems that
seem easy—perhaps the Herrick poems about how flowers got
their colors, the African poem "The Magnificent Bull," and
the American Indian poems. Then, when the children respond
to those, go on to those that seem more difficult. It is important
to remember, though, that children aren't bothered by the
same kinds of difficulties in poetry that adults are bothered by
and aren't bothered in the same way. If children can get the
main feelings of a poem, they won't be intimidated by some
one thing they don't understand. Along the way, they may
even be intrigued by certain kinds of difficulty or strangeness
—Middle English spelling, for example, or words like *thee* and
thou. They have an advantage over some more educated readers whose fear of not understanding every detail of a poem can
keep them from enjoying it at all. Each of these poems has
something that children will like, and which, if the teacher
has a feeling for it too, can make for a good class. These are
also good poems, of course, to teach in junior high and high
school.

I have included a wide variety of poems. I wanted to include enough work by the best poets of the English language to suggest that the great tradition of English and American poetry can be made available to children. Also included are poems in other languages, which children can study in the original or in translation. There are, as well, poems from cultures significantly different from ours: Chinese and Japanese poems and African and American Indian tribal poems.

Cuckoo Song

Sumer is icumen in,
   Lhude sing cuccu!
Groweth sed, and bloweth med,
   And springeth the wude nu—
               Sing cuccu!

Awe bleteth after lomb,
   Lhouth after calve cu;
Bulluc sterteth, bucke verteth,
   Murie sing cuccu!

Cuccu, cuccu, well singes thu, cuccu:
   Ne swike thu naver nu;
Sing cuccu, nu, sing cuccu,
   Sing cuccu, sing cuccu, nu!

This poem has a really happy atmosphere, rather like someone saying "Something's going to happen! Something's going
to happen! Hurrah!" In this poem, it is summer the poet is
excited about, but one could also feel that way about the visit
of a friend, going away on vacation, the end of school, or
Christmas or any other holiday or pleasant time of year. Think
about some exciting thing that you really look forward to and
write a poem about its just beginning to happen. Put in as

211

Cuckoo Song

Summer is a-coming in,
    Sing loud cuckoo!
The seed grows, the meadow blooms
    And the woods spring up now—
                        Sing cuckoo!

Ewe bleats after lamb,
    Cow lows after calf;
Bullock jumps, deer darts about,
    Merrily sing cuckoo!

Cuckoo, cuckoo, you sing well, cuckoo:
    Don't ever stop now;
Sing cuckoo, now, sing cuckoo,
    Sing cuckoo, sing cuckoo, now!

        —translated by Kenneth Koch

many details about it as you can, and include a lot of sounds,
like the cuckoo sounds in this poem. You can address your
poem to a friend or an animal or a bird or even a thing—
"Christmas is on the way! Ring ding, bells!/Oranges in my
stockings! Ding ding!/No kids in school, no homework at home
—Ring ding ding!!!! . . ." It might be good to try to make the
poem more and more excited as it goes along.

Children might enjoy hearing the poem read in Middle English. You can ask them which version sounds more like a cuckoo song. Other things children might like to do in conjunction with this poem and "The Irish Dancer" are to write a poem which sounds like Middle English, or to write a poem in which they put one or two Middle English words in every line. Children are likely to be fascinated by learning that words used to have a different sound and spelling. You might begin by writing some Middle English words on the blackboard (those in the two Middle English poems and other words, too) for the children to use in their poems. They might enjoy using color words, for example, such as *grene, blew, reed, yelwe, purpre;* or more animal-sound words such as *cuccu, bleteth,* and *lhouth.*

The Irish Dancer

Ich am of Irlaunde,
Ant of the holy londe
  Of Irlaunde.
Gode sire, pray ich the,
For of saynte charité,
Come ant daunce wyth me
  In Irlaunde.

The Irish Dancer

I am of Ireland
And of the holy land
  Of Ireland.
Good sir, I pray thee,
For holy charity,
Come and dance with me
  In Ireland.

—translated by Kenneth Koch

Say where you are from, very proudly, and ask someone to come and dance with you there, or sing with you there, or do any other splendid thing you can think of. You might like to make the lines very short, as they are in this poem, which will help give your poem a nice, solid, proud sound, and to repeat some of the words. "I am from Omaha / And from the prairie city / Of Omaha./ My friends, I ask you / To come and do the Twist with me / In Omaha."

Sonetto

Guido, vorrei che tu e Lapo ed io
   Fossimo presi per incantamento,
   E messi ad un vascel, ch' ad ogni vento
   Per mare andasse a voler vostro e mio;

Sicchè fortuna, od altro tempo rio
   Non ci potesse dare impedimento,
   Anzi, vivendo sempre in un talento,
   Di stare insieme crescesse il disio.

E monna Vanna e monna Lagia poi,
   Con quella ch' è sul numero del trenta,
   Con noi ponesse il buono incantatore:

E quivi ragionar sempre d'amore;
   E ciascuna di lor fosse contenta,
   Siccome io credo che sariamo noi.

What if you could have a magic boat (or car or roller coaster or rocketship or plane) and could go anywhere you wanted in it and everything would be perfect? You could have any friends go with you that you wanted. And there would be no work to do and nobody ever to bother you. You could just sail or fly or ride about for as long as you wished, spending every minute with the friends you like best. You could be really close to them and talk about everything and have a good time. Write a poem, like Dante's, inviting your best friend, or saying you wish you could invite him or her, to come with you on such a

Sonnet

Guido, I wish that you and Lapo and I
Were carried off by magic
And put in a boat, which, every time there was wind,
Would sail on the ocean exactly where we wanted.

In this way storms and other dangerous weather
Wouldn't be able to harm us—
And I wish that, since we all were of one mind,
We'd go on wanting more and more to be together.

And I wish that Vanna and Lagia too
And the girl whose name on the list is number thirty
Were put in the boat by the magician too

And that we all did nothing but talk about love
And I wish that they were just as glad to be there
As I believe the three of us would be.

—translated by Kenneth Koch

journey, say what the boat or rocketship or whatever is like, and say what you would do, and who else you would like to come along. (Dante's poem is addressed to his friend Guido Cavalcante; Dante says he would like their friend Lapo Gianni to come along and also their three girlfriends.)—"Bobby, I wish that you and I and Steven / Had a magic balloon which would go anywhere we wanted / And that we could really talk in it as we sailed over Asia and Europe / About the things and people we liked and those we didn't. . . ."

The Demon Lover

"Oh, where have you been, my long, long love,
   This long seven years and more?"
"Oh, I've come to seek my former vows
   Ye granted me before."

"Oh, do not speak of your former vows,
   For they will breed sad strife;
Oh, do not speak of your former vows,
   For I have become a wife."

He turned him right and round about,
   And the tear blinded his ee:
"I would never have trodden on this ground
   If it had not been for thee."

"If I was to leave my husband dear,
   And my two babes also,
Oh, what have you to take me to,
   If with you I should go?"

"I have seven ships upon the sea—
   The eighth brought me to land—
With four-and-twenty bold mariners,
   And music on every hand."

She has taken up her two little babes,
   Kissed them on cheek and chin:
"Oh, fare ye well, my own two babes,
   For I'll never see you again."

She set her foot upon the ship—
　　No mariners could she behold;
But the sails were of the taffeta,
　　And the masts of the beaten gold.

She had not sailed a league, a league,
　　A league but barely three,
When dismal grew his countenance,
　　And drumlie grew his ee.

They had not sailed a league, a league,
　　A league but barely three,
Until she espied his cloven foot,
　　And she wept right bitterly.

"Oh, hold your tongue of your weeping," said he,
　　"Of your weeping now let me be;
I will show you how the lilies grow
　　On the banks of Italy."

"Oh, what hills are yon, yon pleasant hills,
　　That the sun shines sweetly on?"
"Oh, yon are the hills of heaven," he said,
　　"Where you will never win."

"Oh, whaten a mountain is yon," she said,
　　"So dreary with frost and snow?"
"Oh, yon is the mountain of hell," he cried,
　　"Where you and I will go."

He struck the top-mast with his hand,
　　The fore-mast with his knee;
And he broke that gallant ship in twain,
　　And sank her in the sea.

Lord Randal

"O where you have been, Lord Randal, my son?
O where have you been, my handsome young
    man?"—
  "I have been to the wild wood; mother, make my
    bed soon,
For I'm weary with hunting, and fain would lie
    down."

"Who gave you your dinner, Lord Randal, my son?
Who gave you your dinner, my handsome young
    man?"—
  "I dined with my sweetheart; mother, make my bed
    soon,
  For I'm weary with hunting, and fain would lie
    down."

"What had you for dinner, Lord Randal, my son?
What had you for dinner, my handsome young
    man?"—
  "I had eels boiled in broth; mother, make my bed
    soon,
  For I'm weary with hunting, and fain would lie
    down."

"And where are your bloodhounds, Lord Randal, my
    son?
And where are your bloodhounds, my handsome
    young man?"—

"O they swelled and they died; mother, make my
   bed soon
For I'm weary with hunting, and fain would lie
   down."

"O I fear you are poisoned, Lord Randal, my son!
O I fear you are poisoned, my handsome young
   man!"—
   "O yes! I am poisoned; mother, make my bed soon,
   For I'm sick at the heart, and I fain would lie
   down."

These two ballads are story poems, which tell stories by giving
new hints in every few lines about something that has happened or that is going to happen, that only one character
knows about. Lord Randal gradually reveals that he was poisoned by his sweetheart, and the lady in The Demon Lover
gradually finds out that she has made a terrible mistake and
that she is going to hell because the person she went off with
was really a devil and not a man. There are many of these old
ballads and they are usually about serious things like love and
battle and death. They often use repetition, which helps give
a scary and serious effect. Sometimes, like "Lord Randal,"
they are conversation poems between two people. Write a
poem like these in either story or conversation form, about two
people, and have one of the two know something that the other
one doesn't, and give hints about it by what he says or does. He
can give at least one hint in every few lines. For example,
there could be something hidden in a room and one person
knows what it is and the other one doesn't; or one person could
have seen something important (such as a city going up in
flames, or the ocean drying up) which the other person doesn't
know about; or the two people could really be brother and
sister and only one of them knows it; or one could really be a
former friend or sweetheart come back from the dead. It

might be good to decide in advance what the secret, strange and scary thing is which will finally be revealed at the end of the poem. Then you can figure out what hints you'll give in each line or stanza—" 'What is in that room, my dear friend Anne / Which is so bright that its light shines through the walls?' / 'Oh it is only some lights I put there, my friend Jim,/ So that at night we will be able to see.'/ 'But no light is so bright that it shines through walls. . . .' " In this poem the answer could be that what Anne had in the room was the stars or the sun, and that Anne had died and become a spirit who was in charge of lighting the sky.

SIR PHILIP SIDNEY

(ENGLISH, 1554–1586)

Sonnet

Now that of absence the most irksome night,
  With darkest shade doth overcome my day:
  Since *Stella's* eyes, wont to give me my day,
Leaving my Hemisphere, leave me in night,
Each day seemes long, and longs for long-staid night,
  The night as tedious, wooes th' approach of day;
  Tired with the dusty toiles of busie day,
Languisht with horrors of the silent night,
Suffering the evils both of the day and night,
  While no night is more darke then is my day,
Nor no day hath lesse quiet then my night:
  With such bad mixture of my night and day
That living thus in blackest winter night,
  I feele the flames of hottest sommer day.

—from *Astrophel and Stella*

Every line in this poem ends either with the word NIGHT or with the word DAY. It's a love poem. Sir Philip Sidney thinks the girl he loves is like DAY, and her eyes are bright as DAY, and the happiness she could give him is like DAY. But she has gone away, so everything seems like NIGHT—not seeing her is NIGHT, and being unhappy without her is NIGHT. Try a poem like this in which all the lines end in one of two words. It should be a poem about serious feelings. You can use NIGHT and DAY, WINTER and SUMMER, GOLD and SILVER, OKLAHOMA and CALIFORNIA, TRAFFIC LIGHTS and PUERTO RICO, RED and WHITE, or any other words that suggest different kinds of feelings to you. You can

make your poem as complicated and crazy as you like—
"When I see my friend Paul it is SUMMER / But when I have
to stay home alone it is WINTER. . . ." "Having a glass of Coca-
Cola is PUERTO RICO / And flying to Puerto Rico is TRAFFIC
LIGHTS. . . ."

The Passionate Shepherd to His Love

Come live with me and be my love
And we will all the pleasures prove
That valleys, groves, hills, and fields,
Woods, or steepy mountain yields.

And we will sit upon the rocks,
Seeing the shepherds feed their flocks,
By shallow rivers to whose falls
Melodious birds sing madrigals.

And I will make thee beds of roses
And a thousand fragrant posies,
A cap of flowers, and a kirtle
Embroidered all with leaves of myrtle;

A gown made of the finest wool
Which from our pretty lambs we pull;
Fair linëd slippers for the cold
With buckles of the purest gold;

A belt of straw and ivy buds,
With coral clasps and amber studs:
And if these pleasures may thee move,
Come live with me, and be my love.

The shepherds' swains shall dance and sing
For thy delight each May morning:
If these delights thy mind may move,
Then live with me and be my love.

Write a poem in which you try to tempt somebody with all the nicest things you can think of, to convince that person to come and be with you and do things with you. You can say where you would go together, what you would see and hear, what you would do, the gifts you would give. Think about all the things the person would most like to do, and that you would like to do, too. If you like, you can start every line or every two or four lines with "Come with me, and" or words to that effect— "Come with me, and I'll play the guitar for you all day long. . . ."

Over Hill, over Dale

Over hill, over dale
  Thorough bush, thorough brier,
Over park, over pale
  Thorough flood, thorough fire,
I do wander everywhere,
Swifter than the moon's sphere;
And I serve the Fairy Queen,
To dew her orbs upon the green:
The cowslips tall her pensioners be;
In their gold coats spots you see;
Those be rubies, fairy favors,
In those freckles live their savours:
I must go seek some dew-drops here,
And hang a pearl in every cowslip's ear.

—from *A Midsummer-Night's Dream*

Imagine you are very, very small, and you have a special job to do in nature every day. Think about the way something is in nature and imagine that it would only be that way if some little person did something to it every day. There would be a little person, like the one in this poem, to put dewdrops in flowers every morning, one whose job was to keep the grass green, one to make the leaves stick to the branches in summer and make them change color and fall off in autumn, others to do all kinds of things. One could imagine little people like that doing things in a city too—changing the colors of traffic lights, making sure revolving doors go around, putting pretty pictures on stamps in the post office. To have any of these jobs, you would have to be able to move very, very fast and be very active. Imagine you are one of these little people and write a poem about it. You can put one thing you do in every line or make the whole poem about one job you have—"I make sure everyone wakes up in the morning, I tickle their ears / I fly from one place to another, tickling everybody's ears / And I also make sure that daisies and dandelions wake up each morning / I don't tickle them, I give them a little shove with my hand. . . ."

Under the Greenwood Tree

Under the greenwood tree,
  Who loves to lie with me,
  And turn his merry note
  Unto the sweet bird's throat
Come hither, come hither, come hither:
    Here shall he see
    No enemy
But winter and rough weather.

Who doth ambition shun,
  And loves to live i' the sun.
  Seeking the food he eats,
  And pleased with what he gets,
Come hither, come hither, come hither:
    Here shall he see
    No enemy
But winter and rough weather.

—from *As You Like It*

The person singing this song is proud to be out in the country living a simple life—lying under trees, playing music and singing, and living out-of-doors and finding his own food. Did you ever feel proud and happy to be on a camping trip or off in the country somewhere, having a different kind of life from that of your friends back at home? Even if a person didn't really want to stay in the woods or be on the farm forever, he could sometimes feel he wanted to. Write a poem about how nice some kind of life is which is different from your usual life. As in this poem, you can invite certain other people to come share this kind of life with you—"If you like to make your own fires / And cook your own food, even if it's just canned beans / Come live with me by Lake Katonga / And we'll go hiking every day. . . ."

Aubade

Hark! hark! the lark at heaven's gate sings,
    And Phoebus 'gins arise,
His steeds to water at those springs
    On chaliced flowers that lies;
And winking Mary-buds begin
    To ope their golden eyes:
With everything that pretty bin,
    My lady sweet, arise!
        Arise, arise!

—from *Cymbeline*

An aubade is a song which is sung in the morning (it comes from the French word *aube,* which means dawn). In this case, it is sung to wake somebody up. Imagine that you are outside the window of someone who is still asleep. Write a poem telling the person what is happening all around and what he or she is missing by not being awake. If you like, you can start every line with "Listen—" or "Look—" or "You should wake up, because—" "Listen: the birds are singing over on that tree"; "You should wake up—the sun is already shining on the cars!"

Orpheus with His Lute

Orpheus with his lute made trees,
And the mountain-tops that freeze,
Bow themselves when he did sing;
To his music plants and flowers
Ever sprung, as sun and showers
There had made a lasting spring.
Everything that heard him play,
Even the billows of the sea,
Hung their heads, and then lay by.
In sweet music is such art,
Killing care and grief of heart
Fall asleep or, hearing, die.

—from Shakespeare and
Fletcher's *King Henry VIII*

What if you or some other person could sing so beautifully that not only people but also flowers and mountains and oceans and even buildings and cities would listen to the music and be affected by the songs? It would be like having singing as a superpower. At any moment one could use the power of the songs to influence things—to change the weather, to make flowers grow in winter, to make the thunder be quiet, to do all kinds of things. Write a poem about someone who has that power, and tell what he does. It can be you, or someone else. If you like, you can put one magical thing the singer does in every line—"When Sarah sings, she makes the birds be quiet to hear her / And her song makes schools close early so all the teachers and children can listen. . . ."

Listening to songs (recorded or live) may help the children to think of magical things songs could do.

Sonnet

Shall I compare thee to a summer's day?
Thou art more lovely and more temperate.
Rough winds do shake the darling buds of May,
And summer's lease hath all too short a date.
Sometime too hot the eye of heaven shines,
And often is his gold complexion dimmed;
And every fair from fair sometime declines,
By chance, or nature's changing course, untrimmed;
But thy eternal summer shall not fade,
Nor lose possession of that fair thou ow'st,
Nor shall Death brag thou wand'rest in his shade,
When in eternal lines to time thou grow'st.
   So long as men can breathe or eyes can see,
   So long lives this, and this gives life to thee.

Write a very flattering poem about somebody or something, using the kind of "denying comparisons" Shakespeare uses in his poem—"Shall I compare your eyes to the ocean? No, because they're greener and more beautiful than the ocean"; "Should I compare you to an orange? No, you're rounder and oranger than an orange." Try to make the person or thing you're writing about seem as terrific and wonderful as you can.

Shakespeare's poem is also a compliment to himself as a poet, since he says it is this sonnet which will immortalize the person he is writing to. Children might enjoy including a similar theme in their poems—"Jennie, shall I compare you to a tulip?/ You're more beautiful than a tulip!/ And the tulip fades/ But you are lucky, you'll always be beautiful, because of my poem. . . ."

Delight in Disorder

A Sweet disorder in the dresse
Kindles in cloathes a wantonnesse:
A Lawne about the shoulders thrown
Into a fine distraction:
An erring Lace, which here and there
Enthralls the Crimson Stomacher:
A Cuffe neglectfull, and thereby
Ribbands to flow confusedly:
A winning wave (deserving Note)
In the tempestuous petticote:
A carelesse shooe-string, in whose tye
I see a wilde civility:
Doe more bewitch me, then when Art
Is too precise in every part.

Do you like anything that seems sloppy or messy or disorgan-
ized, such as a room with books and cushions all around, or an
unmowed lawn with tall and short grass and weeds and
dandelions, or a sky full of straggly-looking clouds, or a painting full of big splashes and gobs of different colored paint, or
a person with fluffy hair and shirttails out and different colored casual-looking clothes? Write a poem saying what you
like about something like that and maybe also why you like it
more than something absolutely orderly and neat—"I like my
crazy yard full of dandelions and milkweed. / When the wind
blows, the dandelions and milkweed bend on their stems /
And look like people bowing and dancing. / But the yard next
door is always mowed flat green. . . ." "With your hair hanging
loose you look like a movie star. / With your hair up in a bun
you look like Olive Oyl. . . ."

How Violets Came Blew

Love on a day (wise Poets tell)
　Some time in wrangling spent,
Whether the Violets sho'd excell,
　Or she, in sweetest scent.

But *Venus* having lost the day,
　Poore Girles, she fell on you;
And beat ye so, (as some dare say)
　Her blowes did make ye blew.

How Roses Came Red

'Tis said, as *Cupid* danc't among
The *Gods*, he down the Nectar flung;
Which, on the white *Rose* being shed,
Made it for ever after red.

How Marigolds Came Yellow

Jealous Girles these sometimes were,
While they liv'd, or lasted here:
Turn'd to *Flowers*, still they be
Yellow, markt for Jealousie.

These three poems are strange explanations of how flowers
got their colors. Herrick says violets became blue when Venus

hit them, roses became red when Cupid threw nectar on them, marigolds are yellow because they used to be jealous girls and yellow is the color of jealousy (nowadays we think of the color of jealousy as green). Write a poem, or two or three poems, in which you explain how other things got to be the colors they are—flowers, fruits, birds, animals, or the sky, the ocean, the desert, the forest, the stars. You can pretend you were there and saw it happen, or that somebody told you about it. Each poem can be a little story about how one thing got its color, or in every line you can tell how a different thing got its color— "Clouds became white when some girls dressed up for Communion were blown up into the sky"; "Tulips are red, pink, gold, yellow, and purple. / They used to be all white / But one day I saw an airplane carrying a lot of boxes of paints crash against a mountain / And it rained paints and made the tulips all those different colors."

It might be good to bring flowers or fruits to school for the children to look at while they make up their explanations.

Herrick's original spelling has been kept in these four poems so children can see what it is like. The word *then* in the second to last line of "Delight in Disorder" means *than*.

Heaven

O who will show me those delights on high?
      Echo.   I.
Thou Echo, thou art mortall, all men know.
      Echo.   No.
Wert thou not born among the trees and leaves?
      Echo.   Leaves.
And are there any leaves, that still abide?
      Echo   Bide.
What leaves are they? impart the matter wholly.
      Echo.   Holy.
Are holy leaves the Echo then of blisse
      Echo.   Yes.
Then tell me, what is that supreme delight?
      Echo.   Light.
Light to the minde: what shall the will enjoy:
      Echo.   Joy.
But are there cares and businesse with the pleasure?
      Echo.   Leisure.
Light, joy, and leisure; but shall they persever?
      Echo.   Ever.

When you write an Echo Poem you have to pretend you are standing and talking someplace where there is an echo. The echo throws back the sound of the last thing you've said. The things you say are questions, so the sounds the echo throws back seem to be answers. The answers can make sense, as they do in Herbert's poem, or they can be crazy—"How should I act in school? Cool. / What should I eat for Lunch? Unch." Write a poem with a question and an echo answer in every line.

Since echo words may be hard to think of, children may enjoy this more as a class collaboration. Ask for words which have good echo possibilities, such as *table/able, love/of, fall/all, spring/ring, warmer/armor, canoe/new,* and write these on the board. Then ask the children to write lines to go with them. They could call out lines to you, or each could write a poem of his own with the given end-words.

A Song

Ask me no more where Jove bestows,
When June is past, the fading rose;
For in your beauty's orient deep,
These flowers, as in their causes, sleep.

Ask me no more whither do stray
The golden atoms of the day;
For in pure love heaven did prepare
Those powders to enrich your hair.

Ask me no more whither doth haste
The nightingale when May is past
For in your sweet dividing throat
She winters, and keeps warm her note.

Ask me no more where those stars light,
That downwards fall in dead of night;
For in your eyes they sit, and there
Fixèd become, as in their sphere.

Ask me no more if east or west
The phoenix builds her spicy nest;
For unto you at last she flies,
And in your fragrant bosom dies.

Write an exaggerated compliment poem to someone you like
very much, in which you tell where that person gets his or her
nicest characteristics, as Carew says this girl gets her pink

cheeks from the roses, her golden hair from sunbeams, her bright eyes from the stars. If you like, you can make the first line a question, the second an answer, and so on—"Where does the blue of the day go when it's night? / It goes into the blue of your eyes."

WILLIAM BLAKE

(ENGLISH, 1757–1827)

The Lamb

Little Lamb, who made thee?
  Dost thou know who made thee?
Gave thee life & bid thee feed,
By the stream & o'er the mead;
Gave thee clothing of delight,
Softest clothing woolly bright;
Gave thee such a tender voice,
Making all the vales rejoice!
  Little Lamb who made thee?
  Dost thou know who made thee?

Little Lamb I'll tell thee,
  Little Lamb I'll tell thee!
He is called by thy name,
For he calls himself a Lamb:
He is meek & he is mild,
He became a little child:
I a child & thou a lamb,
We are called by his name.
  Little Lamb God bless thee.
  Little Lamb God bless thee.

I taught this together with "The Tyger" and "The Sick Rose" (see Chapter One on teaching Blake).

The Sick Rose

O Rose, thou art sick,
The invisible worm
That flies in the night
In the howling storm

Has found out thy bed
Of crimson joy,
And his dark secret love
Does thy life destroy.

I taught this together with "The Tyger." The poetry idea in that lesson was asking questions of a mysterious and beautiful creature. If this poem is taught alone, though, a more appropriate poetry idea would be telling a flower or tree, or perhaps even a bird or animal, things about itself that it might not know but that the poet knows—"Daffodil, you have three colors in the daytime and one color at night; /Oak tree, you have a squirrel on your branch; /Little cactus, you are all dried up . . ."

SAMUEL TAYLOR COLERIDGE

(ENGLISH, 1772–1834)

Kubla Khan

In Xanadu did Kubla Khan
A stately pleasure dome decree,
Where Alph, the sacred river, ran
Through caverns measureless to man
  Down to a sunless sea.
So twice five miles of fertile ground
With walls and towers were girdled round;
And here were gardens bright with sinuous rills,
Where blossomed many an incense-bearing tree;
And here were forests ancient as the hills,
Enfolding sunny spots of greenery.

But oh! that deep romantic chasm which slanted
Down the green hill athwart a cedarn cover!
A savage place! as holy and enchanted
As e'er beneath a waning moon was haunted
By woman wailing for her demon lover!
And from this chasm, with ceaseless turmoil
  seething,
As if this earth in fast thick pants were breathing,
A mighty fountain momently was forced,
Amid whose swift half-intermitted burst
Huge fragments vaulted like rebounding hail,
Or chaffy grain beneath the thresher's flail;
And mid these dancing rocks at once and ever
It flung up momently the sacred river.
Five miles meandering with a mazy motion
Through wood and dale the sacred river ran,
Then reached the caverns measureless to man,

And sank in tumult to a lifeless ocean;
And mid this tumult Kubla heard from far
Ancestral voices prophesying war!

    The shadow of the dome of pleasure
    Floated midway on the waves;
    Where was heard the mingled measure
    From the fountain and the caves.
It was a miracle of rare device,
A sunny pleasure dome with caves of ice!

    A damsel with a dulcimer
    In a vision once I saw;
    It was an Abyssinian maid,
    And on her dulcimer she played,
    Singing of Mount Abora.
    Could I revive within me
    Her symphony and song,
To such a deep delight 'twould win me,
That with music loud and long,
I would build that dome in air,
That sunny dome! those caves of ice!
And all who heard should see them there,
And all should cry, Beware! Beware!
His flashing eyes, his floating hair!
Weave a circle round him thrice,
And close your eyes with holy dread,
For he on honeydew hath fed,
And drunk the milk of Paradise.

Coleridge said that he was in a sort of trance when he wrote
this poem. He hardly thought at all about what he was writing.

He felt as though the poem were coming to him out of no-where, guiding his pen as he wrote. He felt almost hypnotized. While he was writing, someone knocked on his door and inter-rupted him. When the person left, he wasn't able to get back in the trance-like state again, so he left the poem unfinished.

Close your eyes and try to get in a dreamy state of mind yourself. Picture the strangest, most beautiful place you can possibly imagine. Make it so beautiful you can hardly bear it. Then shut out all other thoughts and try to feel that you're really there, in that place. Write a poem describing the place. You can put in fantastic buildings, fountains, rivers, oceans, mountains, "pleasure domes," "caves of ice," anything. You can tell what you see and how it makes you feel, or you can make your poem a story about the strange and wonderful be-ings who are there and what they do. You might like to use some strange names (real or made-up) as Coleridge does in his poem—Xanadu, Kubla Khan, and Mount Abora—"There is a tower made of red glass in the hills of Aboona / Beside the River Floom whose blue waves would be as silvery as the stars. . . ."

Certain kinds of music on the phonograph might help chil-dren get into a dreamy, Kubla Khan–like state of mind.

GEORGE GORDON, LORD BYRON

(ENGLISH, 1788–1824)

From *Childe Harold's Pilgrimage*

(canto 4)

179

Roll on, thou deep and dark blue Ocean—roll!
Ten thousand fleets sweep over thee in vain;
Man marks the earth with ruin—his control
Stops with the shore;—upon the watery plain
The wrecks are all thy deed, nor doth remain
A shadow of man's ravage, save his own,
When for a moment, like a drop of rain,
He sinks into thy depths with bubbling groan,
Without a grave, unknell'd, uncoffin'd, and unknown.

180

His steps are not upon thy paths,—thy fields
Are not a spoil for him,—thou dost arise
And shake him from thee; the vile strength he
    wields
For earth's destruction thou dost all despise,
Spurning him from thy bosom to the skies,
And send'st him, shivering in thy playful spray
And howling, to his gods, where haply lies
His petty hope in some near port or bay,
And dashest him again to earth:—there let him lay.

181

The armaments which thunderstrike the walls
Of rock-built cities, bidding nations quake,
And monarchs tremble in their capitals,
The oak leviathans, whose huge ribs make

245

Their clay creator the vain title take
Of lord of thee, and arbiter of war;
These are thy toys, and, as the snowy flake,
They melt into thy yeast of waves, which mar
Alike the Armada's pride, or spoils of Trafalgar.

182

Thy shores are empires, changed in all save thee—
Assyria, Greece, Rome, Carthage, what are they?
Thy waters washed them power while they were
    free,
And many a tyrant since: their shores obey
The stranger, slave, or savage; their decay
Has dried up realms to deserts: not so thou,
Unchangeable save to thy wild waves' play—
Time writes no wrinkle on thine azure brow—
Such as creation's dawn beheld, thou rollest now.

183

Thou glorious mirror, where the Almighty's form
Glasses itself in tempests; in all time,
Calm or convulsed—in breeze, or gale, or storm,
Icing the pole, or in the torrid clime
Dark heaving;—boundless, endless, and sublime—
The image of Eternity—the throne
Of the Invisible; even from out thy slime
The monsters of the deep are made; each zone
Obeys thee; thou goest forth, dread, fathomless, alone.

184

And I have loved thee, Ocean! and my joy
Of youthful sports was on thy breast to be
Borne like thy bubbles, onward: from a boy
I wanton'd with thy breakers—they to me

Were a delight; and if the freshening sea
Made them a terror—'twas a pleasing fear,
For I was as it were a child of thee,
And trusted to thy billows far and near,
And laid my hand upon thy mane—as I do here.

Imagine you are friends with some powerful thing in nature
—such as the ocean, the dawn, the mountains, the snow, the
universe, the stars. Think about ways in which this huge
friend of yours is greater than any people could be, greater
than parents, teachers, scientists, presidents, or kings. Write a
poem to ocean-friend or wind-friend or whatever, in which
you tell it how great it is and why—"Stars in the sky, you are
a million times brighter than any fire a man could make. /
Your shining goes further than the most enormous electric
light in the world. / Astronauts go up in rockets but they can
never reach you. / And even if they could they could never put
out your light, you are too powerful. / At night I look up at you
and you look at me, and I smile. Little do they know! . . ."

Personal relationship with a great natural force is also a
theme of "Ode to the West Wind" and "A True Account of
Talking to the Sun on Fire Island." Byron's lines also have
something in common with such poems of exaggerated praise
as "The Magnificent Bull" and "The War God's Horse Song."

Ode to the West Wind

I

O wild West Wind, thou breath of Autumn's being,
Thou, from whose unseen presence the leaves dead
Are driven, like ghosts from an enchanter fleeing,

Yellow, and black, and pale, and hectic red,
Pestilence-stricken multitudes: O thou,
Who chariotest to their dark wintry bed

The wingèd seeds, where they lie cold and low,
Each like a corpse within its grave, until
Thine azure sister of the Spring shall blow

Her clarion o'er the dreaming earth, and fill
(Driving sweet buds like flocks to feed in air)
With living hues and odors plain and hill;

Wild Spirit, which art moving everywhere;
Destroyer and preserver; hear, Oh, hear!

2

Thou on whose stream, 'mid the steep sky's
        commotion,
Loose clouds like earth's decaying leaves are shed,
Shook from the tangled boughs of Heaven and Ocean,

Angels of rain and lightning; there are spread
On the blue surface of thine airy surge,
Like the bright hair uplifted from the head

Of some fierce Maenad, even from the dim verge
Of the horizon to the zenith's height,
The locks of the approaching storm. Thou dirge

Of the dying year, to which this closing night
Will be the dome of a vast sepulcher,
Vaulted with all thy congregated might

Of vapors, from whose solid atmosphere
Black rain, and fire, and hail will burst: Oh, hear!

3

Thou who didst waken from his summer dreams
The blue Mediterranean, where he lay,
Lulled by the coil of his crystalline streams,

Beside a pumice isle in Baiae's bay,
And saw in sleep old palaces and towers
Quivering within the wave's intenser day,

All overgrown with azure moss and flowers
So sweet, the sense faints picturing them! Thou
For whose path the Atlantic's level powers

Cleave themselves into chasms, while far below
The sea blooms and the oozy woods which wear
The sapless foliage of the ocean, know

Thy voice and suddenly grow gray with fear,
And tremble and despoil themselves: Oh, hear!

4

If I were a dead leaf thou mightest bear;
If I were a swift cloud to fly with thee;

A wave to pant beneath thy power, and share

The impulse of thy strength, only less free
Than thou, O uncontrollable! If even
I were as in my boyhood, and could be

The comrade of thy wanderings over heaven,
As then, when to outstrip thy skyey speed
Scarce seemed a vision; I would ne'er have striven

As thus with thee in prayer in my sore need.
Oh, lift me as a wave, a leaf, a cloud!
I fall upon the thorns of life! I bleed!

A heavy weight of hours has chained and bowed
One too like thee: tameless, and swift, and proud.

5

Make me thy lyre, even as the forest is;
What if my leaves are falling like its own!
The tumult of thy mighty harmonies

Will take from both a deep, autumnal tone
Sweet though in sadness. Be thou, spirit fierce,
My spirit! Be thou me, impetuous one!

Drive my dead thoughts over the universe
Like withered leaves to quicken a new birth!
And, by the incantation of this verse,

Scatter, as from an unextinguished hearth
Ashes and sparks, my words among mankind!
Be through my lips to unawakened earth

The trumpet of a prophecy! O wind,
If Winter comes, can Spring be far behind?

Shelley tells the West Wind how powerful he thinks it is, then
asks it to do something for him—to use its power to inspire
him to make him a powerful poet so he can make up poems
that will go all over the world where many people will hear
them. Think of some part of nature—such as wind, the ocean,
the sunlight, the rain, the snow—that has a power that could
help you to get what you want or need. Write a poem in which
you first praise the part of nature—telling it how powerful,
how beautiful, and how marvelous it is—and then ask it to
help you. "Snowflakes, you who can cover the whole city with
white, / You who fall one by one and fall everywhere, / Take
me on your backs and let me be in a thousand places at once,
I want to see everything in the world . . ." "Ocean, you who are
so powerful you can hold up a million ships, / Carry me with
you in your waves and make me almost as powerful as you. /
Let me be a whale in you . . . ."

JOHN KEATS

(ENGLISH, 1795–1821)

Ode on a Grecian Urn

Thou still unravished bride of quietness,
  Thou foster child of silence and slow time,
Sylvan historian, who canst thus express
  A flowery tale more sweetly than our rhyme:
What leaf-fringed legend haunts about thy shape
  Of deities or mortals, or of both,
     In Tempe or the dales of Arcady?
What men or gods are these?What maidens loath?
  What mad pursuit? What struggle to escape?
     What pipes and timbrels? What wild ecstasy?

Heard melodies are sweet, but those unheard
  Are sweeter; therefore, ye soft pipes, play on;
Not to the sensual ear, but, more endeared,
  Pipe to the spirit ditties of no tone.
Fair youth, beneath the trees, thou canst not leave
  Thy song, nor ever can those trees be bare;
     Bold Lover, never, never canst thou kiss,
Though winning near the goal—yet, do not grieve;
  She cannot fade, though thou hast not thy bliss
     Forever wilt thou love, and she be fair!

Ah, happy, happy boughs! that cannot shed
  Your leaves, nor ever bid the Spring adieu;
And, happy melodist, unwearièd,
  Forever piping songs forever new;
More happy love! more happy, happy love!
  Forever warm and still to be enjoyed,
     Forever panting, and forever young;

All breathing human passion far above,
   That leaves a heart high-sorrowful and cloyed,
      A burning forehead, and a parching tongue.

Who are these coming to the sacrifice?
   To what green altar, O mysterious priest,
Lead'st thou that heifer lowing at the skies,
   And all her silken flanks with garlands dressed?
What little town by river or sea shore,
   Or mountain-built with peaceful citadel,
      Is emptied of this folk, this pious morn?
And, little town, thy streets for evermore
   Will silent be; and not a soul to tell
      Why thou art desolate, can e'er return.

O Attic shape! Fair attitude! with brede
   Of marble men and maidens overwrought,
With forest branches and the trodden weed;
   Thou, silent form, dost tease us out of thought
As doth eternity. Cold Pastoral!
   When old age shall this generation waste,
      Thou shalt remain, in midst of other woe
Than ours, a friend to man, to whom thou say'st,
   "Beauty is truth, truth beauty"—that is all
      Ye know on earth, and all ye need to know.

Write a poem in which you talk to the people, animals, and things in a picture or a sculpture. Talk to them as if they might actually be able to hear what you're saying. You can tell them how beautiful or funny or strange they are; you can ask them questions; you can tell them how they make you feel. The best kind of picture or sculpture to look at is one you find really interesting, maybe even mysterious. Most pictures become quite interesting when you look hard at them and try to figure out who the people are and how they feel, and so on—"O girl, you will stand forever in that field/With your horse standing beside you. It's a beautiful horse!/How old is it? What is its name?/I wish I could be there with you in that field/Where the sun shines. I wonder what we would say to each other?. . ." If you're looking at an abstract picture, you can talk to its shapes and colors—"Red, how beautiful you are!/And you, too, Blue, in a big splash right next to Red,/And both of you surrounded by Yellow!/It must be nice to be there with different colors everywhere around. . . ."

This lesson might be made most appealing by bringing to class a picture (or poster or slide) which is at the same time simple and mysterious—something that will make children wonder who the people in it are, what they are thinking and what they are doing. If you want to bring into the children's poems Keats's theme of people staying the same for a long, long time, it would be good if it were a picture from the past, or, perhaps, a picture of a legend.

ROBERT BROWNING

(ENGLISH, 1812–1889)

Home-Thoughts, from Abroad

1

Oh, to be in England
Now that April's there,
And whoever wakes in England
Sees, some morning, unaware,
That the lowest boughs and the brush wood sheaf
Round the elm-tree bole are in tiny leaf,
While the chaffinch sings on the orchard bough
In England—now!

2

And after April, when May follows,
And the whitethroat builds, and all the swallows!
Hark! where my blossomed pear-tree in the hedge
Leans to the field and scatters on the clover
Blossoms and dewdrops—at the bent spray's edge—
That's the wise thrush; he sings each song twice over,
Lest you should think he never could recapture
The first fine careless rapture!
And though the fields look rough with hoary dew,
All will be gay when noontide wakes anew
The buttercups, the little children's dower
—Far brighter than this gaudy melon-flower!

Write a poem about a place you've been—in the country, at the
beach, in another city—or that you've heard about—maybe
Paris, Rome, Africa, China—and where you'd like to be now.

Really think of what it must be like in that place now, and
imagine you can see and hear everything you're imagining. If
you like, put a different thing you imagine happening in the
place in each line. It might be good to talk about the colors and
sounds of different things there, to say what animals and birds
(if any) are there, and what flowers. You may want to start
every line with "I wish" or "I'd like to be" or "Oh, to be . . ."
—"Oh, to be at the beach now, /When the air is just starting
to get warm/And the waves make a loud noise/ And the men
sell pink cotton candy. . . ."

from *Song of Myself*

(section 15)

The pure contralto sings in the organ loft,
The carpenter dresses his plank. . . . the tongue of his
    foreplane whistles its wild ascending lisp,
The married and unmarried children ride home to
    their thanksgiving dinner,
The pilot seizes the king-pin, he heaves down with a
    strong arm,
The mate stands braced in the whaleboat, lance and
    harpoon are ready,
The duck-shooter walks by silent and cautious
    stretches,
The deacons are ordained with crossed hands at the
    altar,
The spinning-girl retreats and advances to the hum
    of the big wheel,
The farmer stops by the bars of a Sunday and looks
    at the oats and rye,
The lunatic is carried at last to the asylum a
    confirmed case,
He will never sleep any more as he did in the cot in
    his mother's bedroom;
The jour printer with gray head and gaunt jaws
    works at his case,
He turns his quid of tobacco, his eyes get blurred
    with the manuscript;
          . . . .

The machinist rolls his sleeves. . . . the policeman

travels his beat. . . . the gatekeeper marks who
pass,

The young fellow drives the express-wagon. . . . I love
him though I do not know him;

The half-breed straps on his light boots to compete in
the race,

The western turkey-shooting draws old and young. . . .
some lean on their rifles, some sit on logs,

Out from the crowd steps the marksman and takes
his position and levels his piece;

The groups of newly-come immigrants cover the
wharf or levee,

. . . .

The bugle calls in the ballroom, the gentlemen run
for their partners, the dancers bow to each other;

The youth lies awake in the cedar-roofed garret and
harks to the musical rain,

The Wolverine sets traps on the creek that helps fill
the Huron,

The reformer ascends the platform, he spouts with
his mouth and nose,

. . . .

The connoisseur peers along the exhibition-gallery
with halfshut eyes bent sideways,

The deckhands make fast the steamboat, the plank is
thrown for the shoregoing passengers,

The young sister holds out the skein, the elder sister
winds it off in a ball and stops now and then for
the knots,

· The one-year wife is recovering and happy, a week
ago she bore her first child,

The cleanhaired Yankee girl works with her
sewing-machine or in the factory or mill,

The nine months' gone is in the parturition chamber,
  her faintness and pains are advancing;
The pavingman leans on his twohanded rammer—
  the reporter's lead flies swiftly over the notebook
  —the signpainter is lettering with red and gold,
The canal-boy trots on the towpath—the bookkeeper
  counts at his desk—the shoemaker waxes his
  thread,
The conductor beats time for the band and all the
  performers follow him,
The child is baptised—the convert is making the first
  professions,
The regatta is spread on the bay. . . . how the white
  sails sparkle!
The drover watches his drove, he sings out to them
  that would stray,
The pedlar sweats with his pack on his back—the
  purchaser higgles about the odd cent,
The camera and plate are prepared, the lady must sit
  for her daguerreotype,
The bride unrumples her white dress, the
  minutehand of the clock moves slowly. . . .

Think about all the different things that are happening right
now in America or in your city or all over the world, and write
a poem with one of these things that's happening in every line.
Really try to think of a lot of things and of many different
kinds of things, and make your poem as long as you can. For
example, you can think about what your parents are doing,
what your friends are doing, what people in different jobs and
in different cities and countries are doing, what babies are
doing, what movie stars are doing, what people on ships and
airplanes are doing, what people in the jungle are doing, what

people at dances and parties are doing, and so on and so on. You can include things that happen in winter, in summer, in the daytime and at night; but write about them all as if they were happening right now—that way the poem will be most exciting—"Children are throwing snowballs at a tree / The airplane pilot brings the 747 down for a landing / The tall girl lies on the beach getting a suntan / The baby is crying in its crib / The coal miner is coming up to fresh air after three days stuck in the mine. . . ."

from *Song of Myself*

(section 26)

I think I will do nothing for a long time but listen,
And accrue what I hear into myself. . . . and let
    sounds contribute toward me.
I hear the bravuras of birds. . . . the bustle of growing
    wheat. . . . gossip of flames. . . . clack of sticks
    cooking my meals.
I hear the sound of the human voice. . . . a sound I
    love,
I hear all sounds as they are tuned to their uses. . . .
    sounds of the city and sounds out of the city. . . .
    sounds of the day and night;

      . . . .

Talkative young ones to those that like them. . . . the
    recitative of fish-pedlars and fruit-pedlars. . . . the
    loud laugh of workpeople at their meals,
The angry base of disjointed friendship. . . . the faint
    tones of the sick,
The judge with hands tight to the desk, his shaky lips
    pronouncing a death-sentence,
The heave'e'yo of stevedores unlading ships by the
    wharves. . . . the refrain of the anchor-lifters;
The ring of alarm-bells. . . . the cry of fire. . . . the
    whirr of swift-streaking engines and hose-carts
    with premonitory tinkles and colored lights,
The steam-whistle. . . . the solid roll of the train of
    approaching cars;
The slow-march played at night at the head of the
    association,

They go to guard some corpse. . . . the flag-tops are
    draped with black muslin.

I hear the violincello or man's heart complaint,
And hear the keyed cornet or else the echo of sunset.

I hear the chorus. . . . it is a grand-opera. . . . this
    indeed is music!

A tenor large and fresh as the creation fills me,
The orbic flex of his mouth is pouring and filling me
    full.

      . . . . . .

The orchestra whirls me wider than Uranus flies,
It wrenches unnamable ardors from my breast,
It throbs me to gulps of the farthest down horror,
It sails me. . . . I dab with bare feet. . . . they are
    licked by the indolent waves,
I am exposed. . . . cut by bitter and poisoned hail,
Steeped amid honeyed morphine. . . . my windpipe
    squeezed in the fakes of death,
Let up again to feel the puzzle of puzzles,
And that we call Being.

This part of "Song of Myself" is all about different sounds,
some of them made by birds, some by fire, by people, by
sticks, by railroad trains, some by people singing or by
musical instruments. Think of all the different sounds you
have heard, or of all the sounds you imagine are being
made now in your city or all over the country, and write a
poem about a lot of these sounds, putting one or more in
every line. You can say what the sounds are like and also

how they make you feel. If you wish, you can start every
line with words like "I hear" or "I listen to"—"I hear the
sound of the train rushing into the station, / I listen to eggs
fry in the pan and to the tinkle of a broken window, / To
the clatter of skates on the sidewalk, to the cry of a crow, to
people calling goodbye. . . ."

I Never Saw a Moor

I never saw a moor,
  I never saw the sea;
Yet know I how the heather looks,
  And what a wave must be.

I never spoke with God,
  Nor visited in heaven;
Yet certain am I of the spot
  As if the chart were given.

Do you ever feel that you really know what something is like even though you've never seen it? Write a poem about some things and people and places you feel sure you know something about in this way. If you wish, the lines could begin with "I never saw" and / "But I know"—"I never saw the city of Paris / But I know what it's like to look up at the Eiffel Tower. / I never saw the inside of a cloud, / But I know what it is like. . . ."

GERARD MANLEY HOPKINS

(ENGLISH, 1844–1889)

God's Grandeur

The world is charged with the grandeur of God.
　It will flame out, like shining from shook foil;
　It gathers to a greatness, like the ooze of oil
Crushed. Why do men then now not reck his rod?
Generations have trod, have trod, have trod;
　　And all is seared with trade; bleared, smeared with
　　　toil;
　　And wears man's smudge and shares man's smell:
　　　the soil
Is bare now, nor can foot feel, being shod.

And for all this, nature is never spent;
　There lives the dearest freshness deep down things;
And though the last lights off the black West went
　Oh, morning, at the brown brink eastward, springs—
Because the Holy Ghost over the bent
World broods with warm breast and with ah! bright
　　wings.

One characteristic of Gerard Manley Hopkins' poems is that
they often get more and more exciting as they go on, as if the
poet were becoming more and more enthusiastic and excited
about what he is saying. This poem, for example, starts with
a direct statement about the world being full of the grandeur
of God. The second and third lines have really exciting images. Then, there's the drum-thump sound of "have trod, have
trod, have trod." Finally, at the end, the poet is so excited that
he interrupts his statement about day and night to say, "Oh!"
and then in the last line right in the middle of looking at the

beauty of the sunrise he says "ah!" when he sees how beautiful
it is. In the same way if you were going swimming and you
were talking while you went into the water and if it shocked
you by being so cold or so nice-feeling, you might say ah! or oh!
or help! in the middle of your sentence: "It really is nice to go
in the oh! water," or "The water is brrr! freezing!" Write a
poem about something you find very exciting. Make it more
and more exciting as you go along. And put in exclamations
like oh! and ah! or hurray! or ouch! or oof! in the middle of
some sentences just to show what you are feeing. You could
also show excitement by repeating words sometimes, such as
"Running, running, running" or "Splashed, splashed,
splashed." "Oh the world looks so beautiful today!/ The wind
is blowing, whoosh! the leaves are swirling hurling furling/
Everywhere! I want to go out and rush through it, / Rushing
rushing rushing, rushing! everywhere! . . ."

(FRENCH, 1854–1891)

Fleurs

D'un gradin d'or,—parmi les cordons de soie, les gazes grises, les velours verts et les disques de cristal qui noircissent comme du bronze au soleil,—je vois la digitale s'ouvrir sur un tapis de filigranes d'argent, d'yeux et de chevelures.

Des pièces d'or jaune semées sur l'agate, des piliers d'acajou supportant un dôme d'émeraudes, des bouquets de satin blanc et de fines verges de rubis entourent la rose d'eau.

Tels qu'un dieu aux énormes yeux bleus et aux formes de neige, la mer et le ciel attirent aux terrasses de marbre la foule des jeunes et fortes roses.

In this short poem Rimbaud mentions eight different colors (gold, grey, green, black, silver, yellow, white, blue); four kinds of fabric (silk, gauze, velvet, satin); nine kinds of metals, wood, stone, and jewels (gold, crystal, bronze, silver, agate, mahogany, emeralds, rubies, marble); and three flowers (foxglove, water rose, and rose). It's as though he were trying to crowd together all the richest, most colorful, most shining and beautiful things he could think of in as small a space as possible. His poem is something like the inside of a jewel box filled with jewels, or the inside of a kaleidoscope. Make lists of your favorite colors, materials, metals, jewels, and flowers, and write a poem about an unbelievably beautiful scene. Put as

Flowers

From a step of gold—amid silk cords, grey gauzes, green velvets, and crystal disks which turn black the way bronze does in the sun—I see the foxglove open on a rug of silver filigree, eyes, and flowing hair.

The water rose is surrounded by yellow gold coins scattered on agate, mahogany pillars holding up a dome made out of emeralds, bouquets of white satin and thin wands of rubies.

Like a god with enormous blue eyes and a body of snow, the ocean and the sky attract the crowd of young and strong roses to the marble terraces.

—translated by Kenneth Koch

many of the items on your lists as possible in every sentence. You can write your poem in lines or you can write it as prose in two or three long sentences. If you like, you can end your poem, as Rimbaud ends his, by suddenly turning from small things to look at big things like the ocean and the sky–"I see gold and silver tulips casting a grey shadow on an enormous pink lace tablecloth with crystal glasses on it and a green agate bowl full of yellow-red oranges and violet-platinum grapes. . . ."

It might be a good idea to make big lists of jewels, flowers, and so on, on the blackboard, with the children calling out suggestions and the teacher writing them down.

WILLIAM BUTLER YEATS

(IRISH, 1865–1939)

Who Goes with Fergus?

Who will go drive with Fergus now,
And pierce the deep wood's woven shade,
And dance upon the level shore?
Young man, lift up your russet brow
And lift your tender eyelids, maid,
And brood on hopes and fear no more.

And no more turn aside and brood
Upon love's bitter mystery;
For Fergus rules the brazen cars,
And rules the shadows of the wood,
And the white breast of the dim sea
And all dishevelled wandering stars.

Imagine you are the ruler of a beautiful magical country, where everyone can be happy forever. Write a poem in which you ask people who seem sad to come and live there where they won't have to worry anymore. You have a magic car or plane to take them there with you. You can tell them in what ways they will be happier. If you like, you can make up a name for yourself, such as Fergus or Angus or The Sun King or the Snow Queen or King Harold or use your own name—"Who will come fly with Steven now/To the country of pink and silver clouds?/We can go there in my magical plane./Everyone talks and dances all day long,/For Steven is the ruler of that cloud place . . ."

Cœur Couronne et Miroir

(heart calligramme) MON CŒUR PAREIL à une flamme renversée

L ES TOUR R OIS Q U I EU A M ENT touR R

RENAISSENT AU CŒUR DES POÈTS

D A N S
F L E T S   C E
R E   M I
L E S   R O I R
S O N T   J E
M E   S U I S
C O M   E N
N O N   Guillaume   C L O S
E T   V I
G E S   Apollinaire V A N T
A N   E T
L E S   V R A I
N E   C O M
G I   M E
M A   O N
I

Heart Crown and Mirror

```
                                              W
      F  L                          T     K        H      H       D
  N        A    M  Y   H            HE    INGS     O      AVE     IED
  W     E      M     E
  O                   A             ONE          BY           onE
  D               R
  E             T                   ARE REBORN IN POETS' HEARTS
  D           L
   I      I
    S    K
     P  E
      U  A
        N
```

```
                    IN    THIS
                IONS          MIR
            FLECT               ROR
             RE                   I
            THE                   AM
            LIKE    Guillaume     EN
            NOT              CLOSED
            AND   Apollinaire  A
            GELS              LIVE
             AN              AND
             GINE         REAL
               MA        AS
                I    YOU
```

—Translated by Kenneth Koch

Think of some happy or sad feeling you have and think of making a poem about it. But imagine you live in a country where all poems are printed as pictures instead of in regular lines, and so you can choose what you think would be the ideal shape for your poem. It can be in any shape at all, but its shape should have something to do with what you're writing about. If your poem is about love, you might want to put it in the shape of the face of the person you love; if it is about rain, it could be rain-shaped or umbrella-shaped; if it is about vague and floaty feelings, it could be in the shape of a cloud—

AND LIGHT WHEN I see you FLOATY ALL feeL I

it could be in the shape of a mountain or of waves—

SOMETIMES I feeL VERY UP AND DOWN LIKE THE waves 'n' THIS SEA POEM

or in the shape of a number—

I WISH I WAS neveR YEARS OLD

It might be easier to draw the outline of the shape first, then mostly erase it. Be sure to make your poem about a real feeling you have.

I'd begin by doing one or two Shape Poems as a class exercise on the blackboard.

D. H. LAWRENCE

(ENGLISH, 1885–1930)

The White Horse

The youth walks up to the white horse, to put its halter
   on
and the horse looks at him in silence.
They are so silent they are in another world.

Write a poem about the quietest things you can think of, things
that make absolutely no noise at all. You can put one quiet
thing in every line or make the whole poem about only one of
them. Lawrence suggests that silence is like another world
because it is as though you were away from the regular world,
where everyone and everything make noise all the time, and
were more in your own dreams. If you wish, you can make
your poem about what a strange effect the silence has, or about
how it makes you feel—"The snow falling on a snowman is so
quiet it makes them both invisible. . . ." "Thinking about my
friend makes me feel quiet, as if I were walking all alone
through space. . . ."

Another way to study this poem is described in the Introduction. If the quietness theme is emphasized, children might
enjoy as part of the same lesson the haiku by Ryota about the
white chrysanthemums. Another approach to these two poems might be sound-color associations. White, in both poems,
seems to suggest silence. You could ask the children if it does
for them too. They could write poems about colors that make
them feel quiet and colors that seem noisy and loud. "The
White Horse" might also be good to study with a noisy poem,
such as "Bantams in Pine-Woods" or "The Cuckoo Song."

Trees in the Garden

Ah in the thunder air
how still the trees are!

And the lime tree, lovely and tall, every leaf silent
hardly looses even a last breath of perfume.

And the ghostly, creamy coloured little tree of leaves
white, ivory white among the rambling greens,
how evanescent, variegated elder, she hesitates on the
    green grass
as if, in another moment, she would disappear
with all her grace of foam!

And the larch that is only a column, it goes up too
    tall to see:
and the balsam pines that are blue with the
    grey-blue blueness of things from the sea,
and the young copper beech, its leaves red-rosy at the
    ends,
how still they are together, they stand so still
in the thunder air, all strangers to one another
as the green grass glows upwards, strangers in the
    silent garden.

Have you ever seen trees or flowers or animals or birds or
people being absolutely still? Write about a scene in which

everything is absolutely unmoving and quiet. If you like, you can put a description of one absolutely still thing in each line—"The cat is absolutely still as she sits on the ground and looks at the yellow bird. / And the bird, too, is absolutely still"; "The clouds don't move; the smoke over the factory doesn't move; the sun doesn't move in the sky."

Humming-bird

I can imagine, in some otherworld
Primeval-dumb, far back
In that most awful stillness, that only gasped and
    hummed,
Humming-birds raced down the avenues.

Before anything had a soul,
While life was a heave of Matter, half inanimate,
This little bit chipped off in brilliance
And went whizzing through the slow, vast, succulent
    stems.

I believe there were no flowers then,
In the world where the humming-bird flashed ahead
    of creation.
I believe he pierced the slow vegetable veins with his
    long beak.

Probably he was big
As mosses, and little lizards, they say, were once big.
Probably he was a jabbing, terrifying monster.

We look at him through the wrong end of the long
    telescope of Time,
Luckily for us.

Have you ever wondered what a small animal, bird, or insect would be like it if were much bigger? Lawrence talks about the hummingbird as a giant, racing monster in a slow, still world of long ago. Imagine you have gone in a time machine back to a primeval world in which creatures now small were very big and powerful, and write a poem about what you see and what you have to do to survive. Say how big things are, what they look like, what kinds of sounds and movements and colors there are. You can make the whole poem mainly about one creature, like a giant hummingbird, or about different ones—"In the otherworld the ants are enormous, each seven feet long / And they are colored not just black and red but also blue / They seem like huge colored lights that dazzle your eyes. . . ."

Der Knabe

Ich möchte einer werden so wie die,
die durch die Nacht mit wilden Pferden fahren,
mit Fackeln, die gleich aufgegangenen Haaren
in ihres Jagens grossem Winde wehn.
Vorn möcht ich stehen wie in einem Kahne,
gross und wie eine Fahne aufgerollt.
Dunkel, aber mit einem Helm von Gold,
der unruhig glänzt. Und hinter mir gereiht
zehn Männer aus derselben Dunkelheit
mit Helmen, die wie meiner unstet sind,
bald klar wie Glas, bald dunkel, alt und blind.
Und einer steht bei mir und bläst uns Raum
mit der Trompete, welche blitzt and schreit,
und bläst uns eine schwarze Einsamkeit,
durch die wir rasen wie ein rascher Traum:
die Häuser fallen hinter uns ins Knie,
die Gassen biegen sich uns schief entgegen,
die Plätze weichen aus: wir fassen sie,
und unsere Rosse rauschen wie ein Regen.

The boy in this poem wishes to be strong and powerful and fast and to go racing through the world on horseback with everything bending before him. Are there any scenes in stories or movies that have made you very excited and made you want to be one of the strong or important people in them? For instance, if you saw or read about an auto racer speeding ahead of everyone else, have you wanted to be him? and have you thought about how that would feel? Or somebody running for a touchdown or leading a parade through the streets with

The Boy

I want to become like one of those
who through the night go driving with wild horses,
with torches that like loosened hair
blow in the great wind of their chasing.
Forward I want to stand as in a skiff,
large and like a flag unfurled.
Dark, but with a helm of gold that glints
uneasily. And in a row behind me
ten men out of the selfsame darkness
with helmets that are as unstaid as mine,
now clear as glass, now dark and old and blind.
And one beside me stands and blasts us space
upon his trumpet that flashes and that screams,
and blasts us a black solitude
through which we tear like a rapid dream:
the houses fall behind us to their knees,
the streets bend slantingly to meet us,
the squares give way: we take hold of them,
with our horses rushing like a rain.

—translated by M. D. Herter Norton

confetti flying and the band playing, or swimming very fast
through the waves to get to an island before anyone else?
   Write a poem about wanting to be somebody like that in a
scene you've seen or a story you've read, and how you imagine
it would feel—"I want to be like a dangerous cowboy on a swift
horse /Who rides through one town after another / And who
even rides swiftly through the mountains / As though he were
flying and the mountains were big bunches of clouds. . . ."

Aus einer Kindheit

Das Dunkeln war wie Reichtum in dem Raume,
darin der Knabe, sehr verheimlicht, sass.
Und als die Mutter eintrat wie im Traume,
erzitterte im stillen Schrank ein Glas.
Sie fühlte, wie das Zimmer sie verriet,
und küsste ihren Knaben: Bist du hier? . . .
Dann schauten beide bang nach dem Klavier,
denn manchen Abend hatte sie ein Lied,
darin das Kind sich seltsam tief verfing.

Er sass sehr still. Sein grosses Schauen hing
an ihrer Hand, die ganz gebeugt vom Ringe,
als ob sie schwer in Schneewehn ginge,
über die weissen Tasten ging.

From a Childhood

The darkening was like riches in the room
in which the boy, withdrawn and secret, sat.
And when his mother entered as in a dream,
a glass quivered in the silent cabinet.
She felt how the room had given her away,
and kissed her boy: Are you here? . . .
Then both gazed timidly towards the piano,
for many an evening she would play a song
in which the child was strangely deeply caught.

He sat quite still. His big gaze hung
upon her hand which, all bowed down by the ring,
as it were heavily in snowdrifts going,
over the white keys went.

—translated by M. D. Herter Norton

This poem is about a very special time in someone's child-
hood, a very quiet and private time which meant a lot to him,
when he and his mother would be all alone in the evening and
she would play the piano for him. Can you remember any time
like this when you were younger, when you felt especially
close to someone or felt very happy and quiet about something? It could be a time, for example, when you were alone
in bed at night, or talking to a friend after you were in bed, or
walking with your dog, or sitting looking at your cat, or being
smiled at by a certain person. Usually people keep such feelings secret because they feel embarrassed about them or because they think no one else has such feelings and so wouldn't
understand. But probably everyone has them. Write a poem
about an experience like this that you've had. If you want to
stress the secretness of it, you could begin some of the lines
with words like "I've never told anyone how much I liked" or
"I secretly liked." The poem can be about one expreience or
about different ones—"I secretly always was happy when my
uncle would take me for a walk /He would come in the house,
in winter, shaking the snow off his coat / And he would take
my hand and walk with me outside in the cold day . . ."

WALLACE STEVENS

(AMERICAN, 1879–1955)

Anecdote of the Prince of Peacocks

In the moonlight
I met Berserk,
In the moonlight
On the bushy plain.
Oh, sharp he was
As the sleepless!

And, "Why are you red
In this milky blue?"
I said.
"Why sun-colored,
As if awake
In the midst of sleep?"

"You that wander,"
So he said,
"On the bushy plain,
Forget so soon.
But I set my traps
In the midst of dreams."

I knew from this
That the blue ground
Was full of blocks
And blocking steel.
I knew the dread

Of the bushy plain,
And the beauty
Of the moonlight
Falling there,
Falling
As sleep falls
In the innocent air.

Write a poem about meeting a strange person or creature in a strange, frightening, beautiful place full of colors and having a conversation with him or it. If you like, your poem can be about a dream, as Stevens's seems to be. The meeting can take place in a weird landscape full of steel and bushes, as in Stevens's poem, or in a boat on a sea of blue paint—any strange place at all. In Stevens's poem, the person he meets and talks to is called "Berserk," which is not really anyone's name but a word that means "crazy." You can give the person or creature you talk to a name which is just a word too. If you like, you can begin the poem by saying where you met the person or creature and then make the rest of the poem the things you say to each other. "On a mountain made of emeralds, I met Impossible—he looked snow-covered / I said, Why are you covered with snow? / He said, Because I am red and green . . ."

Disillusionment of Ten O'Clock

The houses are haunted
By white night-gowns.
None are green,
Or purple with green rings,
Or green with yellow rings,
Or yellow with blue rings.
None of them are strange,
With socks of lace
And beaded ceintures.
People are not going
To dream of baboons and periwinkles.
Only, here and there, an old sailor,
Drunk and asleep in his boots,
Catches tigers
In red weather.

Write a "Not Poem" in which you describe something and
then give a lot of examples of what it is not, as Stevens does
here with the night-gowns. Think of strange, impossible, and
perhaps beautiful things which you would like to be there but
which aren't. You might like using short lines like Stevens's
lines—"In school / Everyone wears black or brown shoes. /
None are silver, with yellow bows, / None are made of glass
so they sparkle in the light, / None are made of purple butterfly wings. . . ."; "My house has two storys and is made of
wood. / Its windows and doors and steps are all even and
straight. / It has no heart-shaped windows, full of sparkly
sunlight, / And no doors shaped like a polar bear, / And no
stairs which curve . . ."

Bantams in Pine-Woods

Chieftain Iffucan of Azcan in caftan
Of tan with henna hackles, halt!

Damned universal cock, as if the sun
Was blackamoor to bear your blazing tail.

Fat! Fat! Fat! I am the personal.
Your world is you. I am my world.

You ten-foot poet among inchlings. Fat!
Begone! An inchling bristles in these pines,

Bristles, and points their Appalachian tangs,
And fears not portly Azcan nor his hoos.

This is a poem about a little bantam rooster meeting up with
an Indian chieftain and telling him off. The chief has a lot of
feathers just as the rooster does and looks to him like a great
big rooster. But the bantam isn't at all afraid of him. The most
noticeable thing about the poem is the way it sounds (and how
hard it is, at first, to understand). Actually the words sound
something like the noises an angry rooster might make. Write
a poem full of wild and crazy-sounding words which sounds
like an angry or excited speech by some kind of bird or animal
or by some kind of thing that makes noises, such as a whistle
or a train. You could make it a speech by one creature or thing
or a conversation between several or between you and it. Don't
only use animal noises like woof woof and bow wow but try to
find regular words that sound the way a creature does too. If

it's a dog, for example, you could have lines like "Don't get rough, rough, and crowd, crowd my bark off the roof! Woof!" If it's a canary—"Tweet! Big feet! I was trying to sleep, when you leaped past the seat, meat feet!"

It may be helpful to put lists of words on the board that sound like the noises different creatures make—with the children supplying most of them, of course.

The Wood-Weasel

emerges daintily, the skunk—
don't laugh—in sylvan black and white chipmunk
regalia. The inky thing
adaptively whited with glistening
goat-fur, is wood-warden. In his
ermined well-cuttlefish-inked wool, he is
determination's totem. Out-
lawed? His sweet face and powerful feet go about
in chieftain's coat of Chilcat cloth.
He is his own protection from the moth,

noble little warrior. That
otter-skin on it, the living pole-cat,
smothers anything that stings. Well,—
this same weasel's playful and his weasel
associates are too. Only
Wood-weasels shall associate with me.

Write a poem about an animal, bird, or insect you like but that
somebody else you know doesn't like—or that most people
don't like. Tell what you like about it in a sort of tough sassy
way. You can also tell the person or people you're writing the
poem to why the creature you're writing about is better than
they are. Like Marianne Moore, you can use the first words of
the poem as the title—"MY WHITE MICE / are delicate and light
and quick / They look like ping-pong balls with feet / They
have eyes as pink as cotton / candy. They are more affection-
ate than you. . . ."

Something you could include in your poem is a description

of the creature's looks as if it were wearing clothes made out
of other creatures—Marianne Moore describes the skunk as
wearing "chipmunk regalia," "goat-fur," "ermined" and "cut-
tle-fish-inked wool," a "coat of Chilcat cloth," and "otter skin."

Or you could make a separate poem out of that kind of description of one or more creatures—"THIS BEETLE / has a black
oyster-shell / overcoat and this squirrel has a little mink coat.
This rabbit is wearing a / white angora-wool bunny-suit. . . ."
As in the poem and in these examples, you could try to end
your lines in surprising places, not at the end of sentences.

LÉOPOLD SÉDAR SENGHOR

(WEST AFRICAN, 1906–)

Je veux dire ton nom

(pour tama)

Je veux dire ton nom Naëtt! Je veux te psalmodier
    Naëtt!

Naëtt, son nom a la douceur de la cannelle c'est le
    parfum où dort le bois de citronniers.
Naëtt, son nom a la blancheur sucrée des caféiers en
    fleurs
C'est la savane qui flamboie sous l'amour mâle de
    Midi.
Nom de rosée plus frais que l'ombre et le tamarinier
Plus frais que l'éphémère crépuscule quand se taît
    la chaleur du jour.

Naëtt, c'est la tornade sèche et l'éclat dense de la
    foudre.

Naëtt louis d'or charbon de lumière ma nuit et mon
    soleil
Moi ton champion je me suis fait mâbo pour te
    nommer
Princesse d'Elisse qu'exila le Fouta par un jour de
    désastre.

I Want to Say Your Name

I want to say your name, Naëtt! I want to make you
   an incantation, Naëtt!

Naëtt, her name has the sweetness of cinnamon it's
   the perfume where the wood of lemon trees
   sleeps.
Naëtt, her name has the sugared whiteness of coffee
   trees in flower
It's the savannah which blazes beneath the
   masculine love of the mid-day sun.
Name of dew cooler than shade and the tamarind
   tree
Cooler than the quickly-passing dusk when the heat
   of day is silenced.

Naëtt, it's the dry whirlwind and the dense clap of
   thunder.

Naëtt coin of gold coal of light my night and my sun
I your champion I have made myself a sorcerer to
   name you
Princess of Elissa exiled from Fouta on a
   catastrophic day.

Write a poem about a person whose name you like and about
all the things the name makes you think of. Think of what
colors the name is, what time of year it makes you think about,
what metal it is like, what kind of clothing. Is it like an ocean?

a lake? like mountains? like the sky? Does it make you think of any cities or countries? "Joanne your name is orange, / It makes me think of peach trees, / It makes me think of gold coins floating in the sea. . . ."; "I will say your name, Richard! It is strong as steel / It is as cold and beautiful as sea gulls flying a million miles away / It is a day in winter, in February, when everything is white and blue. . . ." If you like, you can talk about a different name in every line.

Cirque d'Hiver

Across the floor flits the mechanical toy,
fit for a king of several centuries back.
A little circus horse with real white hair.
His eyes are glossy black.
He bears a little dancer on his back.

She stands upon her toes and turns and turns.
A slanting spray of artificial roses
is stitched across her skirt and tinsel bodice.
Above her head she poses
another spray of artificial roses.

His mane and tail are straight from Chirico.
He has a formal, melancholy soul.
He feels her pink toes dangle toward his back
along the little pole
that pierces both her body and her soul

and goes through his, and reappears below,
under his belly, as a big tin key.
He canters three steps, then he makes a bow,
canters again, bows on one knee,
canters, then clicks and stops, and looks at me.

The dancer, by this time, has turned her back.
He is the more intelligent by far.
Facing each other rather desperately—
his eye is like a star—
we stare and say, "Well, we have come this far."

Write a poem about a favorite toy or doll or stuffed animal. Write about it as though it were something important that people should know about, as if you were doing an eyewitness news report. Tell the world what the doll or toy looks like, what it's made of, what it is doing at the moment (or what you imagine it is doing), what it is probably thinking and feeling —"The teddy bear is eighteen inches tall / His fur is as brown as a desk in school / His eyes are black buttons smaller than a dime / On his feet are attached two wheels / He rolls toward me halfway across the floor and stops. . . ." If you like, at the end, you or the toy or doll, or both, can say something—"Well, I am much smaller than you this year"; "Last night while you were asleep there was a snowstorm."

Piano and Drums

When at break of day at a riverside
I hear jungle drums telegraphing
the mystic rhythm, urgent, raw
like bleeding flesh, speaking of
primal youth and the beginning,
I see the panther ready to pounce,
the leopard snarling about to leap
and the hunters crouch with spears poised;

And my blood ripples, turns torrent,
topples the years and at once I'm
in my mother's lap a suckling;
at once I'm walking simple
paths with no innovations,
rugged, fashioned with the naked
warmth of hurrying feet and groping hearts
in green leaves and wild flowers pulsing.

Then I hear a wailing piano
solo speaking of complex ways
in tear-furrowed concerto;
of far-away lands
and new horizons with
coaxing diminuendo, counterpoint,
crescendo. But lost in the labyrinth
of its complexities, it ends in the middle
of a phrase at a daggerpoint.

And I lost in the morning mist
of an age at a riverside keep
wandering in the mystic rhythm
of jungle drums and the concerto.

Do different kinds of music make you feel different ways? This African poet, Gabriel Okara, says that drums make him feel that he's a little boy, and in the jungle with the wildness and the trees and the animals. And that European piano music makes him feel very different things—subtle and complicated, civilized things. Write a poem about the ways two different kinds of music, or two different musical instruments, make you feel. If you like, you can write the first line about one kind of music, the second about the other kind, and so on—"The Beatles' records make me feel like jumping up and throwing my arms around / But organ music makes me feel like a heavy cloud floating in the sky. . . ."

Music on records, or live music played on different instruments, could be helpful with this lesson.

Les Étiquettes Jaunes

I picked up a leaf
today from the sidewalk.
This seems childish.

Leaf! you are so big!
How can you change your
color, then just fall!

As if there were no
such thing as integrity!

You are too relaxed
to answer me. I am too
frightened to insist.

Leaf! don't be neurotic
like the small chameleon.

Jaune is the French word for *yellow*. *Étiquettes* is the French word for the little white tags that are put on things in stores to show price, size, and so on. *Étiquette* also means what it does in English: the proper way to behave. Frank O'Hara doesn't think the leaf is behaving properly by turning yellow and falling off the tree.

Think about something you've seen a leaf or a flower or a plant do—or, if you prefer, a bird or fish or insect or animal—which is a perfectly natural thing for it to do, but which would be a strange thing to do if it were a person. Write a poem to it as if it were a person and tell it why you're bothered or surprised by what it is doing—"Rose! you're so red! Why do you close up your petals at night? / Isn't that rather rude? What if somebody wanted to talk to you? . . ."; "Snowflakes! What's the idea of melting and turning into water? / Don't you want to be the same person for two days in a row? / Turn back into snowflakes! . . ."

A True Account of Talking
to the Sun at Fire Island

The Sun woke me this morning loud
and clear, saying "Hey! I've been
trying to wake you up for fifteen
minutes. Don't be so rude, you are
only the second poet I've ever chosen
to speak to personally
                              so why
aren't you more attentive? If I could
burn you through the window I would
to wake you up. I can't hang around
here all day."
                    "Sorry, Sun, I stayed
up late last night talking to Hal."

"When I woke up Mayakovsky he was
a lot more prompt" the Sun said
petulantly. "Most people are up
already waiting to see if I'm going
to put in an appearance."
                              I tried
to apologize "I missed you yesterday."
"That's better" he said. "I didn't
know you'd come out." "You may be
wondering why I've come so close?"
"Yes" I said beginning to feel hot
wondering if maybe he wasn't burning me
anyway.
            "Frankly I wanted to tell you

I like your poetry. I see a lot
on my rounds and you're okay. You may
not be the greatest thing on earth, but
you're different. Now, I've heard some
say you're crazy, they being excessively
calm themselves to my mind, and other
crazy poets think that you're a boring
reactionary. Not me.
                Just keep on
like I do and pay no attention. You'll
find that people always will complain
about the atmosphere, either too hot
or too cold too bright or too dark, days
too short or too long.
                If you don't appear
at all one day they think you're lazy
or dead. Just keep right on, I like it.

And don't worry about your lineage
poetic or natural. The Sun shines on
the jungle, you know, on the tundra
the sea, the ghetto. Wherever you were
I knew it and saw you moving. I was waiting
for you to get to work.

                And now that you
are making your own days, so to speak,
even if no one reads you but me
you won't be depressed. Not
everyone can look up, even at me. It
hurts their eyes."
                "Oh Sun, I'm so grateful to you!"

"Thanks and remember I'm watching. It's

easier for me to speak to you out
here. I don't have to slide down
between buildings to get your ear.
I know you love Manhattan, but
you ought to look up more often.

        And
always embrace things, people earth
sky stars, as I do, freely and with
the appropriate sense of space. That
is your inclination, known in the heavens
and you should follow it to hell, if
necessary, which I doubt.

        Maybe we'll
speak again in Africa, of which I too
am specially fond. Go back to sleep now
Frank, and I may leave a tiny poem
in that brain of yours as my farewell."

"Sun, don't go!" I was awake
at last. "No, go I must, they're calling
me."

    "Who are they?"

        Rising he said "Some
day you'll know. They're calling to you
too." Darkly he rose, and then I slept.

What if all the big parts of nature—like the sun, the moon, the
stars, the mountains, the snow, the thunder, the air, spring-
time—suddenly became able to talk and went around talking
to people they especially liked? The sun in this poem likes
Frank O'Hara because he thinks he is warm and loving and
generous like himself, the sun. Which big part of nature would
you most want to like you and come and talk to you? Write a

poem about it happening and what you two would say to each other. Think about how it really would be to be with someone as warm and bright and powerful as the sun, or as cold and mysterious and glamorous as the snow. Any nice thing it said to you would really be wonderful. The things it liked about you would probably be characteristics it had too—" 'Alice,' the Air said, as she seated herself on the edge of my bed,/'I like you because you're so light and easy the way I am—' / (It was getting very breezy in the room but I didn't say anything—) / 'And I like the way you go to a lot of different places to see and do things. . . .' "

This relatively casual way of talking about serious things to a great natural force might be enjoyable for children after they study the more formal invocations—to the ocean and to the West Wind—of Byron and Shelley.

The Painter

Sitting between the sea and the buildings
He enjoyed painting the sea's portrait.
But just as children imagine a prayer
Is merely silence, he expected his subject
To rush up the sand, and, seizing a brush,
Plaster its own portrait on the canvas.

So there was never any paint on his canvas
Until the people who lived in the buildings
Put him to work: "Try using the brush
As a means to an end. Select, for a portrait,
Something less angry and large, and more subject
To a painter's moods, or, perhaps, to a prayer."

How could he explain to them his prayer
That nature, not art, might usurp the canvas?
He chose his wife for a new subject,
Making her vast, like ruined buildings,
As if, forgetting itself, the portrait
Had expressed itself without a brush.

Slightly encouraged, he dipped his brush
In the sea, murmuring a heartfelt prayer:
"My soul, when I paint this next portrait
Let it be you who wrecks the canvas."
The news spread like wildfire through the buildings:
He had gone back to the sea for his subject.

Imagine a painter crucified by his subject!
Too exhausted even to lift his brush,
He provoked some artists leaning from the buildings
To malicious mirth: "We haven't a prayer
Now, of putting ourselves on canvas,
Or getting the sea to sit for a portrait!"

Others declared it a self-portrait.
Finally all indications of a subject
Began to fade, leaving the canvas
Perfectly white. He put down the brush.
At once a howl, that was also a prayer,
Arose from the overcrowded buildings.

They tossed him, the portrait, from the tallest of the
    buildings;
And the sea devoured the canvas and the brush
As though his subject had decided to remain a
    prayer.

This poem has a strange form: it is a sestina, and all its lines end with the same six words. The six words here are BUILDINGS, PORTRAIT, PRAYER, SUBJECT, BRUSH, and CANVAS. Sestinas can use all kinds of end-words. There is another sestina by John Ashbery with the end-words THUNDER, APARTMENT, COUNTRY, PLEASANT, SCRATCHED, and SPINACH (it is a sestina about Popeye). Students at PS 61 wrote a class sestina in which all the end-words were colors: PINK, AQUAMARINE, GREEN, BLUE, PURPLE, and RED. A sestina can tell a story, as "The Painter" does, or it can be about different places or wishes or dreams or anything else. Choose six words that you would like to use a lot and write a sestina with these as end-words. Or you can do it as a class collaboration, with the whole class deciding on words and someone writing the words and then the lines to go with them on the blackboard.

This is probably best done, the first time anyway, as a class collaboration. Ask students to choose the end-words, which you then write on the board in the proper order. Then call on different children for lines to fit the end-words. The traditional order of the end-words is 123456, 615243, 364125, 532614, 451362, 246531. In each of the three final lines there are two end-words, and the order is 12/34/56. For examples of children's sestinas and more details about the form, see *Wishes, Lies, and Dreams,* pp. 216–223. Children might enjoy writing on their own a shorter version of the sestina—a poem of only twelve or eighteen lines, for example, using each end-word only two or three times. Sidney's "Sonnet" is a good poem to teach in the same series of lessons.

FOUR CHINESE POEMS

CH'U YUAN

(TWELFTH CENTURY, B.C.)

In Praise of the Orange Tree

Fairest of all God's trees, the orange came and settled
    here,
Commanded by Him not to move, but grow only in
    the south country.
Deep-rooted, firm and hard to shift: showing in this
    his singleness of purpose;
His leaves of green and pure white blossoms delight
    the eye of the beholder,
And the thick branches and spines so sharp, and the
    fine round fruits,
Green ones with yellow ones intermingled to make a
    pattern of gleaming brightness.
Orange on the outside, but pure white within, the
    fruits yield a parable for human conduct!
Rich and beautiful, his loveliness is not impaired by
    any blemish.

Oh, your young resolution has something different
    from the rest.
Alone and unmoving you stand. How can one not
    admire you!
Deep-rooted, hard to shift: truly you have no peer!
Awake to this world's ways, alone you stand,
    unyielding against the vulgar tide.
You have sealed your heart; you guard yourself with
    care; have never fallen into error.
Holding a nature free from selfishness, you are the
    peer of heaven and earth.

I would fade as you fade with the passing years, and
    ever be your friend.
Pure and apart and free from sin, and strong in the
    order of your ways:
Though young in years, fit to be a teacher of men;
In your acts like Po Yi: I set you up as my model.

                 —from *The Nine Declarations,*
                 translated by David Hawkes

Write a poem about a tree or plant or flower or fruit that you
like. Imagine that it is a person—what good qualities would it
have? An oak tree looks as though it would be big and strong
and honest and dependable. A tulip looks bright and fresh and
sort of perky—it would probably be a cheerful friend and
somebody nice to dance with or go shopping with. A birch tree
looks rather elegant and distinguished. A pine tree looks
rather sturdy and tough, since it never loses its greenness, and
one could imagine that it liked sports and other outdoors
things since it stays on the mountains in the far North even
in winter. A watermelon looks sort of jolly and easygoing,
probably fun to gossip with. In your poem, if you like, you can
put one good quality of the tree or plant or flower in every line.

    The first half of the Chinese poem is written *about* the
orange tree. In the second half the poet talks to the orange tree
as if it were a person who could understand him. You could do
that in your poem too.—"The clover is gentle and quiet and
pink and white and it grows in this meadow"; "Oh, your easy
way of standing in the meadow, Clover, makes people feel
peaceful and happy. . . ."

Oath of Friendship

SHANG YA!
I want to be your friend
For ever and ever without break or decay.
When the hills are all flat
And the rivers are all dry,
When it lightens and thunders in winter,
When it rains and snows in summer,
When Heaven and Earth mingle—
Not till then will I part from you.

—*translated by Arthur Waley*

In Yüeh, the part of China where this poem was written, when men made friends with each other they set up an altar of earth and had a ceremony during which they recited this oath. Write a Friendship Oath of your own to your best friend or to a new friend or to someone you want to be friends with. Imagine you are outside at a ceremony, saying it out loud. If you like, you can say in every line how long you will like your new friend. Or you can say what you will do for him. Or how much you like him—"I want to be friends with you till we are one hundred years old / Till you have a long white beard"; "If we are friends, I will give you my clothes to wear"; "My friend, I will like you more than I like eating and drinking."

Eating Bamboo Shoots

My new province is a land of bamboo-groves:
Their shoots in spring fill the valleys and hills.
The mountain woodman cuts an armful of them
And brings them down to sell at the early market.
Things are cheap in proportion as they are common;
For two farthings, I buy a whole bundle.
I put the shoots in a great earthen pot
And heat them up along with boiling rice.
The purple nodules broken—like an old brocade;
The white skin opened—like new pearls.
Now every day I eat them recklessly;
For a long time I have not touched meat.
All the time I was living at Lo-yang
They could not give me enough to suit my taste,
Now I can have as many shoots as I please;
For each breath of the south-wind makes a new
      bamboo!

—translated by Arthur Waley

Write a poem about eating or drinking. Think of something
you love to eat or drink. Think of everything you like about it
—its taste, its smell, the way it feels, the way it looks. Imagine
that you are living in a place where there is so much of this
food that you can have all of it you want—it's everywhere—
and you never get tired of it. It can be peaches growing in trees
all around your house, or wonderful lemonade or rootbeer
coming out of fountains in your room. Say in your poem what

the food (or drink) is, where you find it, how much it costs (if anything), how you eat or drink it (do you cook it? do you eat it in your fingers or with a knife and fork? do you drink it from a glass or do you dip your face into it and drink?). Try to make anyone who reads your poem really hungry or thirsty for what you write about—"My street is a street filled with raspberry bushes. / Raspberries grow along the sidewalk and in window boxes and on people's roofs. / They even grow in the street— sometimes raspberries stop traffic! / They are red and pink and slightly bumpy and they taste like the sweetest cool water you can imagine. / I eat them in big handfuls and stain my wrists with their juice. . . ."

from *Cold Mountain*

6

Men ask the way to Cold Mountain
Cold Mountain: there's no through trail.
In summer, ice doesn't melt
The rising sun blurs in swirling fog.
How did I make it?
My heart's not the same as yours.
If your heart was like mine
You'd get it and be right here.

7

I settled at Cold Mountain long ago,
Already it seems like years and years.
Freely drifting, I prowl the woods and streams
And linger watching things themselves.
Men don't get this far into the mountains,
White clouds gather and billow.
Thin grass does for a mattress,
The blue sky makes a good quilt.
Happy with a stone underhead
Let heaven and earth go about their changes.

8

Clambering up the Cold Mountain path,
The Cold Mountain trail goes on and on:
The long gorge choked with scree and boulders,
The wide creek, the mist-blurred grass.
The moss is slippery, though there's been no rain
The pine sings, but there's no wind.

Who can leap the world's ties
And sit with me among the white clouds?

—translated by Gary Snyder

Think about a place which is like the way you feel sometimes. If it is a happy feeling, it might be a place full of flowers and little streams and fruit trees and lots of birds. If it's a sad feeling, it might be a gloomy cave. If it's an excited feeling, it might be all jagged mountain crags and vast views of distant landscapes and oceans. If it's a quiet, peaceful feeling it might be the quiet, velvety inside of a flower. Write a poem about such a "mood-place" and give it a name, like Cold Mountain or Daffodil Street. You can say what it's like there, how you get there, how long you have been there or when you go there, what kind of other person could go there with you (if you like, you can make the whole poem an invitation to someone to come there and visit you)—"When I go to my Gloomy Jungle, everything is dark and monkeys are jumping around"; "In my secret garden everything is quiet—the colors are pink, red, yellow, and white"; "On Dreamy Mountain everything is blurred and misty. / If you like everything to be clear, don't come there. / But if you like strange shapes of clouds, come and see me there. . . ."

FIVE JAPANESE POEMS

SHIKI

(1867–1902)

What a wonderful
day! No one in the village
doing anything.

—*translated by Harry Behn*

ISSA

(1763–1829)

Wild goose, wild goose,
At what age
Did you make your first journey?

—*translated by Kenneth Rexroth*

RYOTA

(1718–1787)

No one spoke,
The host, the guest
The white chrysanthemums.

—*translated by Kenneth Rexroth*

The old pond;
A frog jumps in—
    the sound of the water.

    —translated by R. H. Blyth

With what voice,
And what song would you sing, spider,
    In this autumn breeze?

      —translated by R. H. Blyth

Writing very short poems is like making a drawing with only three or four lines. If you choose the right lines or words, you can get some very pleasant and strange effects. These five haiku show various ways of writing very short poems.

"What a wonderful day! . . ." Begin with a general statement, then give a surprising reason for it—"How happy I am! I couldn't go to sleep last night"; "New York is beautiful! Fire-plugs gleaming in the sunlight!"

"Wild goose. . . ." Ask a bird or animal a question which could seem silly but which you really might want to ask anyway— "Brown squirrel, brown squirrel, are you happier running up or running down the tree?" "Goldfish, as you grow older, do you feel you know more than you did before?"

"No one spoke. . . ." Make a list with one surprising thing in it (in this list the surprising thing is the chrysanthemums, since no one would expect them to speak anyway) and make it secretly some kind of comparison between people and something in nature—"I have three friends: Jane, Sarah, and a maple tree."

"The old pond. . . ." Describe something one way, then have something happen, and describe the same thing another way —"The large brick school building. Three o'clock comes. The sound of screaming and of bells."

"With what voice. . . ." Begin with a regular question you might ask a person, but ask it of something surprising, such as an insect—"If you had all the money in the world, what would you buy with it, mosquito?"

———

I'd suggest ignoring syllable count when teaching children haiku. Like rhyme, it restricts them in a bad way. The inspiring thing here is shortness and quickness, making a whole poem out of only a few words, which these haiku show various ways to do. Children may wish to write their poems as one line or to divide them into two or three lines. They might enjoy writing a number of haiku in one class.

The Magnificent Bull

My bull is white like the silver fish in the river
white like the shimmering crane bird on the river
    bank
white like fresh milk!
His roar is like the thunder to the Turkish cannon on
    the steep shore.
My bull is dark like the raincloud in the storm.
He is like summer and winter.
Half of him is dark like the storm cloud,
half of him is light like sunshine.
His back shines like the morning star.
His brow is red like the beak of the Hornbill.
His forehead is like a flag, calling the people from a
    distance,
He resembles the rainbow.

I will water him at the river,
With my spear I shall drive my enemies.
Let them water their herds at the well;
the river belongs to me and my bull.
Drink, my bull, from the river; I am here
to guard you with my spear.

Dinka tribe

This poet is really proud of his bull. It seems as though he is
comparing him to everything he can think of that is strong
and beautiful and shining—to a fish, to a crane, to milk, to

cannon, to a cloud, to summer and winter, to sunshine, to a star, to a bird's beak, to a flag, and to a rainbow. Write a poem like this about something or someone you think is absolutely great—it can be your dog or cat, your favorite tree or river or mountain or building, your favorite baseball or football player or team, your favorite animal or person of any kind. In every line say how amazingly wonderful the person or creature or thing is. Exaggerate the way you would in an argument about who had the best dog or the most beautiful garden, or the best or most beautiful anything. Whether it's really completely true or not, compare what you write about to the moon, the sun, the stars, air, water, animals, birds, and so on. You might like to try to sound the way you think a tribesman would sound, standing outside saying his poem out loud, or singing it—"My dog is as golden as the sun. / When my dog runs he makes the sound of the north wind in the forest. / My dog's bark is as loud as the engines of one hundred jet planes or fifty volcanoes. . . ."

This seems to be a poem meant to have a magic effect, like the three Indian poems which follow, and children may be intrigued by the similarities. In its magical use of praise it seems related also to "Ode to the West Wind." A similar extravagance in making comparisons can be seen in some of the Blake poems by the children from Swaziland, as well as in their Comparison Poems and Noise Poems.

Song for the Sun
That Disappeared behind the Rainclouds

The fire darkens, the wood turns black.
The flame extinguishes, misfortune upon us.
God sets out in search of the sun.
The rainbow sparkles in his hand,
the bow of the divine hunter.
He has heard the lamentations of his children.
He walks along the milky way, he collects the stars.
With quick arms he piles them into a basket
piles them up with quick arms
like a woman who collects lizards
and piles them into her pot, piles them
until the pot overflows with lizards
until the basket overflows with light.

Hottentot tribe

Think about a rainstorm or a snowstorm or a big wind blowing
or an eclipse or a very hot day, and imagine that there are
super-beings in the sky who are trying to bring things back to
normal, just as the god in this poem wants to get rid of the
darkness and so goes out to collect stars in a basket to make the
world light again. Write a poem which tells the story of how
the super-being (or super-beings) changes what is happening
so that it gets better in the world. If you like, you can tell one
thing the super-being does in each line—"On a suffocatingly
hot day in August, the Rainbow Bird goes looking for rain ice
cubes. / She finds them in Venus's refrigerator and melts them
in the heat of the sun, so it rains and we cool off. . . ."

Dawn Song

(from the Gotal Ceremony)

The black turkey in the east spreads his tail
The tips of his beautiful tail are the white dawn

Boys are sent running to us from the dawn
They wear yellow shoes of sunbeams

They dance on streams of sunbeams

Girls are sent dancing to us from the rainbow
They wear shirts of yellow

They dance above us the dawn maidens

The sides of the mountains turn to green
The tops of the mountains turn to yellow

And now above us on the beautiful mountains it is
    dawn.

    —Mescalero Apache; adapted from P.E. Goddard

Love-charm Song

1

I can charm that man
I can cause him to become fascinated

2

What are you saying to me?
I am dressed in colors of the roses?
and as beautiful as the roses?

3

I can make him bashful
I do wonder what can be the matter with him
that he is bashful?

4

I can do this where he may be
under the earth
or in the very center of the earth!

—Ojibwa; adapted from Densmore

The War God's *Horse Song*

I am the Turquoise Woman's son

On top of Belted Mountain beautiful horses
slim like a weasel

My horse has a hoof like striped agate
his fetlock is like fine eagle plume
his legs are like quick lightning

My horse's body is like an eagle-feathered arrow

My horse has a tail like a trailing black cloud

I put flexible goods on my horse's back

The Holy Wind blows through his mane
his mane is made of rainbows

My horse's ears are made of round corn

My horse's eyes are made of stars

My horse's head is made of mixed waters
    (from the holy waters)
    (he never knows thirst)

My horse's teeth are made of white shell

The long rainbow is in his mouth for a bridle

with it I guide him

When my horse neighs
different-colored horses follow

When my horse neighs
different-colored sheep follow

I am wealthy from my horse

Before me peaceful
Behind me peaceful
Under me peaceful
Over me peaceful
Around me peaceful
Peaceful voice when he neighs
I am everlasting and peaceful
I stand for my horse

—Navajo; adapted from Dane
and Mary Roberts Coolidge

These three poems are special poems to be chanted or sung at
special times. Many American Indian tribes have songs and
poems like these to go with special occasions. Such songs are
often partly magic, sung in order to help make things happen.
The song which describes the beautiful dawn may help to
make sure that the dawn will come again and again. The
love-charm song, in which the woman tells how irresistible
she is, is supposed to make her irresistible to a man so he will
fall in love with her. The horse song, which says how wonderful the war god's horse is, may be partly to get the help of the
war god, before a battle, partly to make sure one's horse will
be fast and strong. The songs are full of praise and boasting

—the idea behind this is that if you say how good and strong and beautiful something is, it will help it to be that way. It's like wishing, but instead of saying you wish something were true you say it *is* true—instead of saying "I wish I could win the bicycle race," you say "My bicycle is faster than all the other bicycles in the world and wins every race."

Imagine what it would be like if, like the Indians, you had special poems or songs for the important things in your life— a sunrise poem for the morning, a poem about how wonderful your report card is to make sure you get good grades in school, a poem to make sure you do well in some game. A poem to sing before a baseball game, for example, might start like this: "I am the greatest baseball player in the world. / My arms are as strong as battering rams and as fast as electricity. / When I swing my bat the wind blows for a thousand miles. . . ." (Such a song actually would probably make you feel pretty good about the game.) Write one or more poems like these for special occasions.

Some Poems from Swaziland

Before they wrote their Blake poems, Peace Corps worker Mary Bowler's students in Swaziland wrote a number of poems suggested by the poetry ideas in *Wishes, Lies, and Dreams.* She sent these to me, and they seemed to me so good and so interesting that I wanted to include them in the next book I wrote about children and poetry. Aside from their excellence and their interest as poems by children from a different culture, these poems may be useful to teachers as examples of poems about wishes, comparisons, and so on, to read to their students to help inspire them in writing their own. The vividness and originality of the Swazi poems are likely to have a good effect. The poetry ideas used are Wishes, Comparisons, Noises, I Used To/But Now, Lies, If I Were the Rain, and Poems Using Words in Another Language. My PS 61 students wrote poems about being the snow, but being the rain seemed a better idea for Swaziland, where it rains but doesn't snow. My students used Spanish words in their other-language poems; Mary Bowler had hers use color words in siSwati, the native language of Swaziland.

WISH POEMS

I wish a man to have wings and fly like a dove with
    blue and white and red.
I wish to have two heads brown and white like a
    monster.

I wish to have a brown dog with a long mouth and
    short legs and the stomach could touch down so
    that the mouth could be fed.

I wish I had a big white bird which would fly up into
heaven and come back with good colored feathers
used by the Angels of God.

I wish I had a pink monkey with eight tires not legs.

I wish the people of the United States of America do
not know the black millpity which has a hundred
legs.

I wish to have a car with some black flying birds
near it.

I wish to be a great grey kangaroo so that I would use
the pouch as my lovely bag.

I wish to have a black cat with long broad ears so
that when it walks the ears could touch down
and hear when the ants sing.

I wish if the blue sea will vanish and I see all the
animals.

I wish all the white colored animals God bless.

I wish I will be a bed covered with brown paper like
a chimpanzee that drinks cocoa every day and
plays football every Friday.

I wish green forests to vanish so that I can catch
bucks.

I wish I was a man with a variegated face, black and
white like a monkey.

I wish all green mouses to have no teeth for eating
    our maize.

I wish all green mambas to have no poison when it
    bites somebody must not die.
I wish to have a red bicycle so that I might give it to
    my dog.

I wish to have a black donkey which has three legs
    and no tail so that I can laugh at it.
I wish to have a blue chair so that my black cat will
    sit on it.

I wish to have a blue cow so that I can eat blue meat.

I wish the old people to be like brown animals of the
    forest and have four legs, hands and feet turn to
    paws.
I wish to have a black donkey so I could see a red
    flame in its nose during the night.
I wish I were the black and white bird with the sweet
    voice.

I wish my black cat could carry my water can.

I wish to see a white man like a buck with long eyes
    and tongue to touch the earth's surface.

I wish I had a yellow and white peacock so that I
   could see it when it sprang its wings.
I wish to have a cat and bear a child which is like a
   white angel and the cat carry the child to heaven.
I wish to be white so that I can be the white stork.

I wish to die so that I may see the blue heaven and
   stay with the eagle.
I wish to have a blue cow that crows in the morning.

I wish my black cat could talk so that I must call it
   and talk together.
I wish a black dog to born a lion of one leg and one
   eye.

I wish the blue sky to fall and see above the heavenly
   animals.

I wish my green dog to fly in the air in order to catch
   the birds.
I wish to see an animal with a dark brown beard.

I wish to have a green dog which is a million men.
I wish to have a brown snake which has no teeth on
   it.
I wish to see a brown lion with five heads and two
   legs.

I wish the animals would be changed to short men.
I wish to kill black and white zebra when I am well
   known.

The students of St. Mary's Secondary School

COMPARISON POEMS

Learning is like a key for your room to open.
Absalom is as still as a door nail.
I am as beautiful as a white angel going to heaven.
My hair is as black as coal.
The red sunlight coming out is as pretty as my sister.

To live in a luxury way is like to live in heaven.
John is thin like a small stick which can easily
   break.
The cow is like a frog jumping deep in the water.
John is like a black wizard that I saw in the dark
   night.
Rivers are as long as veins.

Miss Bowler is beautiful like a golden fish that lays
   eggs on the doors of heaven, which have a white
   back for carrying angels.
To be angry is like the brown hungry puff adder in
   the bush.
Happiness is like a dead person going to heaven.

Swaziland is a green watered country like Paradise.
Learning at school is like buying a golden egg.

Death is like the sleepy door nail.
That girl is as thin as a wasp's waist.
Crying for your dead son is like the whole world
    crying for hunger during the times of war.
Doing things without looking for your future is like
    going into the darkness of your life.

The future of a person is like a new plant planted in
    the warm fertile place.
The King's feet are like Jesus' feet when walking
    upon the sea with three blue stars following him.
Ploughing young crops in the good place is like a
    good child of a Christian family.
Passing at school is as good as a golden eagle sitting
    on your head.
My white dog's eyes are glittering as gold and marble
    in the doors of heaven.

Today the sun shines as brightly as a new pin.
Love is like flying in the atmosphere.
Learning is like you are preparing a way to heaven.
Stephen is as tall as a giraffe eating leaves from the
    bush.
Sugar is as tasty as honey.

Sleeping is like going by train to the Transvaal and
    coming back in the same day.

"Ah" is as big as an elephant in the forest.
My head is like a fish as it swims in water.
Winning at Casino is like seeing the moon shining at
    night.
Getting cordial greetings is like finding a purse full
    of money.

My black eagle is almost as quick as lightning.
Amos is like an angry black lion ready to catch
    something.
Nine, ten, eleven were running as fast as a man who
    is chased by a red lion.
The King's palace is so attractive like a palace of
    King Midas who lived in England many years
    ago.
The American teachers are so kind like the angels of
    heaven.

Tomorrow the sun will shine like a rainbow from the
    sky.
My father's first son is like a bright angel flying
    across the blue sky.
Sleeping at night is like buying a swallow that lays
    golden eggs.

My face is as black as coal.
Miss Bowler is as pretty as flowers.
Irma is as tall as a giant.
My father is as wise as King Solomon.
Evelyn is beautiful as a silent black cat.

I am beautiful like an angel coming from the heaven
with a shining face.
Waking at dawn is like seeing the birds of heaven.
People during the war cry like the thunder of the
heaven.
John's head is as big as a blue ball.

Saul's teeth are black like a grasshopper's teeth.
Dreaming is like swimming in a blue deep ocean.
Hope is as promising as the red rising sun.
The Bishop's eyes are rolling like a watch.

Christianity is as big as the planet Jupiter.
The American flag on the moon is as forlorn as a
pelican perched on the Pacific Ocean.

The students of St. Mary's Secondary School

NOISE POEMS

A noise made by a train is like a noise made by wild
pigs in the big forests of the Amazon basin.
A noise that is made by a lion is like a noise made by
a bomb.
The noise of my car is like the noise of Apollo 12
when it was going to the moon.
The noise made by the rain is like the people
whistling the whistle for the King at the stadium.

The heart pumping sounds like the pumping tube of
a car.

Crying sounds like monkeys chattering in the bush.
The sound made by rivers is like the blood running
inside the veins.
The noise made by a mosquito is like the sound made
by a cat running after a mouse.
The noise made by a watch sounds like a cat trying
to catch a bird.
The noise made by a plastic bag is like a bat crying
at night.

Coughing when you have T.B. sounds like a zebra
roaring in the forest.
Scratching yourself sounds like a cat going to catch a
rat.
A noise made by an American teacher when teaching
is like a noise made by the angels from heaven.
Wind in the trees sounds like rain.
A noise made by some cars sounds like the noise of
small chickens.

The sound of a pot boiling is like the sound of a
chimney in the factory.
The sound of paper is like the pilot machine flying
up to the sky.
The ring of the bell sounds like the sing of the birds.
Water falling from a rock sounds like a heavy wind.
The noise which is made by the lion is like the roar
of thunder.

The thunderstorm is like a sound made by an atomic
bomb.
The noise of folding paper is like the sound of
washing.
Sleeping people sound like whistling trains and
hoarse frogs.
The sound of moving bees is like many people
drinking in the hotel.
Today the trees hiss like a snake trying to catch a
frog.

Weeping of a monkey sounds like the crying of a
young baby.
Wind sounds like a jet plane playing over the valleys
of heaven.
Playing a guitar sounds like God calling his angels.
The noise that is made by dancing is like a man in a
hurry drinking tea.
The noise that is made by trains is like the sound of
your heart when it is pumping blood.

The sound of crying is like the sound of nearly
touching the heaven's door.
Running very fast sounds like a herd of cattle going
to the river to drink water.
Kicking a football sounds like the moving water of
the sea.
The noise of folding paper quickly is like the fat put
in the hottest pot.

The noise of a happy person is like the noise of birds
enjoying the warm weather in summer.
The noise made by a horse sounds like the noise of a
huge giant.
The noise made by a thunderstorm sounds like the
roaring of a lion.
The noise of the tractor is like the noise of a rocket to
the moon.
A lion sounds like a thunderstorm when it starts to
rain.

Crying is like a group of people dancing in the hall.
The crying of a baby is like the buzzing of a bee.
Shaking some beans in a bottle sounds like the frogs
when croaking.
The spray of a deodorant can sounds like water
falling at Mantenga Falls.
The sound made by the ducks is like a person
coughing.

The sound that is made by the ocean is like the
sound that is made by the ducks when they are
crying.
Playing a saxophone sounds like a person crying in
hell.
The noise of a printing machine sounds like small
birds in the bush.
A frog sounds like a dull baby crying.

When you are putting out a fire it sounds like the
smoking of a train.

This class is noisy like the men coming to drink beer.
The noise made by the phone sounds like the bell of
  a bicycle.
Plastic paper sounds like a puff adder wobbling
  through a valley of flowers.

The noise made by the American flag on the moon
  sounds like the angels' trumpets coming with
  peace on earth.
Rustling leaves sound like German soldiers on
  parade.
Hisses of snakes sound like a time bomb ready to
  explode.
Boiling water sounds like a puff adder taking off to
  bite a person.

When my mother bought me some shoes, they made
  a happy noise that sounds like a bird when
  singing up on top of a tree looking down at all
  the wonders of the world.

The clock sounds like a Swazi person saying "no, no,
  no."

The students of St. Mary's Secondary School

DREAM POEMS

In my dream I saw the door of heaven open and I
  saw a man sitting on the throne.
The throne was made of gold and silk.
There were seven brave lions surrounding the throne.
He was holding a stick in his hand and his eyes were
  as red as fire and his hair as white as snow.

In my dream I was near the badge of Swaziland.
The lion said, "Let peace abide in this country."
The Elephant said, "Let Swaziland have a
  progressive life."
And then I heard the voice of a man crying in the
  wilderness.

In my dream I dream an enormous city ablaze.
In one of the tall buildings, children screaming;
People jumping through windows.
Policemen, cars, firemen running up and down the
  streets.
Long red flames pointing up into the blue sky.
To men, the world seemed to be ending.

In my dream my father likes gold better than
  anything else in the world.

My father went to the garden and he touched the
    cabbage and it changed to gold.
In the house he touched the table; everything in the
    house changed to gold.
He touched my little sister and she changed to gold.
When my father cried he himself changed to gold.

In my dream I saw King Sobhuza II visiting my
    house.
I boiled tea for him, but he didn't drink it.
After that I saw myself with him going to the
    Holiday Inn for he wanted to drink beer.

In my dream I saw my grandfather rising from
    death.
He was telling me how they stay in heaven.
I asked him when will he come back to stay with us.
While I was asking my father, the angel of God lifted
    him up and he disappeared.

In my dream I saw four cows eating food sitting at a
    table using forks and knives.
I came to ask the owner of the house about the
    strange sight.
The cows simply disappeared in the view.

The students of St. Mary's Secondary School

LIE POEMS

I will not die. Instead I will turn to a space ship
    which will be the fastest in the world.
A headmaster should sweep all the classrooms and
    his office.
Percy Sledge is the Father of Soccer and Cassius Clay
    is a magician.
Cows eat meat and I eat grass.
The storekeeper gives people bread every morning.

Students must teach and teachers must listen.
One day I went to school with the sun. When I was in
    class the sun laughed at us learning how to read
    and write.
I sleep with my cow in my bed.
A school child must drink beer not milk.
A rich man eats porridge and sugar whereas a poor
    man eats porridge and meat every day.
I used to speak English when I have drunk beer.

Europeans wear long dresses and Africans wear mini
    dresses.
The first man to land on the moon was Percy Sledge.
The clouds are the story carriers to heaven.
For supper I eat ice cream from the library.
Once I marry a black American girl I will take her to
    live in safety on the moon.

The Zulus live in Swaziland. They always like to eat
   dogs and they keep bucks for hunting them.
I once met a cat. One day it told me that it was going
   to stay on the moon because it is tired of staying
   here on the earth.

The floor is a brown cat which creeps under the
   ground.
I think Miss Bowler will marry the white angel that
   will give her a white ape.
I was surprised when King Sobhuza landed on the
   moon with his black bearded face.
My ears are 6 feet long and my head is like a
   hexagon that has 6 sides.

My arm is made of iron. When I ring it all the
   children come and wait for assembly.
I am wearing a hat on my leg and a trouser on my
   arm.
The sun is 2 inches long and 1 inch wide.
Our principal is Augustine and my classmate is Mr.
   Simeland.

Blankets of Americans are made out of snow.
My school is built on a heavy dark cloud above the
   sky. The headmaster of it is a strong wind.
Once I put my feet in my pockets and my hands in
   my shoes.
The first person to land on the moon was traveling by
   bicycle.

The man who brought education was wearing a
    swallow-tailed coat.
Augustine left his tail at home this morning. That's
    why he's got trousers on.

Nowadays there's no need to pray because our
    ancestors prayed for their generations.
The Americans teach fish how to fly to the moon.
The Americans are the fish of the Atlantic Ocean
    who made the Indian Ocean for the Portuguese to
    build their bank in the center.
The thunder is made by lions when roaring, asking
    God to give them food.
Teachers are illiterate people.

Every Sunday I visit the sun.
While I am there I eat nothing . . .
But the flame made by the sun.
When I am about to leave the sun
I make a supper of crabs and potatoes
And start my Apollo back to my country.
When I arrive back after five hours away
All the fishes come out from the water
And dance with me as the first girl to visit the sun.

On Monday the King told us that the Mdzimba
    Mountain will move from Lobamba to Manzini.
After hearing that all the birds flew away from
    Swaziland to America.
There are no more birds in Swaziland.
But now all the dogs have been changed to birds.

And the Mdzimba Mountain is no more at Lobamba
   but at Manzini.

I live on the moon with ghosts.
They have taught me their language.
Our food is dried frogs.
We sleep in fire without a blanket.
Our horses are fat flies . . . we ride them.

In Swaziland rivers run uphill and mountains are
   falling.
In Swaziland the Houses of Parliament are built on
   fig trees.
In Swaziland we eat bricks and drink air.
In Swaziland cats wear trousers and Swazis have fur.
In Swaziland cocks make the laws and human beings
   live in rocks.

Clouds in the morning come from my house.
Clouds are eaten by the sun as it rises.
Clouds visit me in the morning.
Clouds are my morning food.
Clouds drive away monkeys from the forest in the
   morning.
Clouds in the morning are like the Zulu army
   attacking the White Man in Africa.

The students of St. Mary's Secondary School

I USED TO/BUT NOW POEMS

I used to be an outlaw
But now I've hung my guns.

I used to be a hard studier
But now I've gone mad.

I used to be a driver of a motorcycle
But now I am nothing else but a grasseater.

I used to be a man walking with four legs.
But now I am a boy with ten legs flying in the air.

I used to be an angel that gave children gifts on
    Christmas
But now I'm Santa Claus with a big, white marvelous
    beard.

I used to be a witch doctor with lots of pollutions in
    my gourds.
But now I'm a magician playing in a dark river
    among crocodiles.

I used to be ten hungry devils
But now I am ten lions roaring in the dark forest.

I used to be a bird flying over the blue oceans of the
     world
But now I am a crocodile boating in the rivers of
     Swaziland.

I used to be a football player
But now I am one of the Commonwealth runners of
     Swaziland.

I used to be a skeleton
But now I am a person.

I used to be a woman
But now I am a man.

I used to be in love with many boys
But now I'm in love with one boy.

I used to be so big like an elephant
But now I am as lean as bacteria germs.

I used to marry lobsters.
But now I am a school child.

I used to stay with angels
But now I am a star.

I used to be a lion that goes like an old woman going
    to bed
But now I do not because my legs are broken.

I used to see golden flowers in my dreams
But now I can't.

I used to be Prime Minister
But now I am a poor man.

I used to be a baboon staying in the forest
But now I am a man living in the moon.

I used to pray in Church
But now I sneak behind the cross.

I used to be beaten every month
But now I am the King of Soccer.

I used to be a fisherman
But now I buy fish from the store.

I used to be a red Indian girl who did not like
    plaiting her hair
But now I am a fairy who likes flying above the sky.

I used to be a wide mouth
But now I am long legs.

I used to be a good person for my age
But now I am a palm tree.

I used to be a person who depends on mother's breast
But now I depend on delicious food I need.

I used to be a pilot of the American airplane
But now I am one of the pilots of the Swaziland
    trains.

I used to be a wild dog
But now I am a poor puff adder.

I use to be hungry at quarter past twelve
But now I'm satisfied.

I used to be a lover of lobsters
But now I am a lover of ants.

I used to live in New York
But now I live in Swaziland.

I used to be as tall as a giraffe
But now I am as short as a chair.

I used to be a mother of small chickens who always
    cried for some food and I, as a mother, ran to and
    fro.
But now I am free, for all the chickens have grown
    up and they are mothers too.

I used to jump all the way home
But now I walk perfectly.

I used to be a jockey
But now I am a pianist.

I used to be a priest
But now I am a wizard.

I used to be a rock but now I am a part of the King's
    palace.

I used to be a priest converting natives of the world
But now I am a drunkard drinking beer all days and
nights emptying hundreds of drums an hour.

I used to be a screamer every morning
But now I'm always shining like a sun.

I used to be a best fighter
But now I am a Tsotsi girl.

I used to be a dog to catch rabbit for my father
But now I am a chair for him.

I used to play in forests
But now I play on the streets.

The students of St. Mary's Secondary School

*POEMS ABOUT
BEING THE RAIN*

Up above in the cooler layers of the atmosphere
It's where my residence is.
I contribute generously
I come down on the parched grass and trees.

I'm able to dissolve problems.
I wake all things from their dormant states.
I dissolve the earth's surface.
I fill rivers with water
Which provide men and animals with me.

Living things show their beautiful faces.
Trees with their variegated colors.
Maize fields with their white hairs.
I'm proud of myself.

Through the veins of the earth I flow
Providing life to fishes and crocodiles.
I also show my rainbody which is part of my body.
God bless me and you.

Augustine Magongo

In the big dark clouds I drift,
The country down below becoming dark under my
    shadow.
Here and there children shouting after cattle;
Some yelling for other children.
Children, parents gather into houses,
The moment I begin to fall.
Some despise, some congratulate,
Of course life depends on me.
Dropping down from the above heaven
I feel so light—of course lighter than a feather.
With a sudden drop onto the ground
It swallows me in two shakes of a duck's tail.

Stephen Dennis

After the dry seasons of Swaziland
Up in the sky I prepare my way to come down
And water the dry land of Swaziland.
When I am about to fall down
I first appear as dark clouds coming
From the east of Swaziland.

After that I fall down in little drops as pure waters of
     heaven.
In order to be fierce I thunder
As if the doors of heaven are opened.
When I am tired of pouring water
I stop and make a rainbow stretching from the east
     to the west.
I am pretty and my waters are sweet as the sweet
     drink of Swaziland.

Catherine Nhlengethwa

When I was a rain I was drizzling
People with houses with corrugated iron roofs put out
     their buckets so that I could fall in.
They use me for cooking foods.
They drink me.
They use me for their washings.
When they do all these things I become unhappy.
But God made me for that.
You can't do anything without me, Miss Rain.
I am one of the wonders of the world.

Frances Sibiya

When I fall down the chickens eat me thinking that I
am maize.

When I fall down an old woman takes me thinking
that I am a five cent piece.

When I fall down the children take me and put me in
their tins.

When I fall down all people wear their raincoats and
their hats.

When I fall down poor people who have no hats and
raincoats their hair becomes white and their
clothes become wet.

When I fall down all the cattle are driven to the
kraal.

When I fall down hens, chickens, and cocks fold their
wings and put their chickens under them.

Irma Thomo

If I come to rain in Swaziland
I come rushing on mountains,
Birds are flying so high and are so happy.
When I fall on the ground some creatures are not so
happy.
They hide themselves in holes and die there.
But frogs are so happy after rain,
And they begin to sing their song . . .
Kroo, kroo, kroo.
Trees are green during that time.

Nehemiah Ndimande

The First Rain of Swaziland
After the Great Drought

When I start forming clouds
People and animals hope of the rain which I am
    going to give them.
If I start thundering and lightening and shifting
    ground and destroying houses and so, they fear
    me and hide themselves
Praying in dark corners for help from God.

When I rain I go in every place except some places
    which are covered up like houses.
After some few minutes I stop thundering and
    raining.
Rivers and valleys full of water going down the slope.
Birds and animals coming out singing in different
    voices.
Frogs can be seen after I have passed, singing and
    jumping in the rivers.
Grass growing every animal feeding itself.
Mothers holding their hoes in the fields.
Men putting yokes on oxen to plough in their fields.
Mothers putting their babies on their backs, following
    the oxen.
All that they are doing is because I, the rain, have
    come.

Author unknown

POEMS USING siSWATI WORDS

The Story of Mankaiana

Mankaiana is a mnyama town and there are many
    mnyama and bomvu people who live there.
One day I saw one mtfubi man.
He walked with the luhlata girl.
The people of Mankaiana were jealous when they
    saw that beautiful luhlata girl.
My brother who is mnyama also liked the luhlata
    girl.
The mtfubi man beat my brother.
My brother turned to mhlophe and lubedze colors.
My father beat the man.
My poor father turned to nkomi color.
The Mankaiana people were very angry.
In return they beat the magic mtfubi man.
But they all turned to mafatsafatsa colors.

I saw a man spitting mhlophe water.
And all the street of Manzini became mhlophe.
Later, looking down through the enkangala
Beautiful birds chattering with bomvu and mhlophe
    colors
I remember my father in Joburg.
A black visage, that is mhyama khwishi,
Reminds me of my black cow grazing in the luhlata
    grass of heaven.

Oh! Mnyama, mnyama isn't that African beauty?
Those bright bomvu flamingoes swiftly pass by like a
Luthulu, mthubi cloud, bringing a bomvu terrific roll
   of thunder.

A bomvu, mthubi, luhlata daisy flower attracts a
   msundu little bee.

I wonder why the grass is luhlata,
And why the bomvu wind is never seen.
Who taught the mnyama necked bird to build a nest,
And the bomvu, luhlata trees to stand still and rest.

A luhlata cow hears a mhlope sound and
It runs with its nsundu hooves.
It got a bomvu band on a hlaza thorn.
The cow cried mthubi tears.

I heard a mhlophe town crying,
Mnyama and mhlophe and bomvu people for liberty.
Luhlata tears falling from their eyes.
Crying bomvu, mnyama and mhlophe in mhlophe
   town of Manzini.

My lovely mnyama bird
Flying over the luhlata sea,
The mpunga fish caught its sight
The bomvu helicopter picked it up.

Month June is muthubi in color,
The lovely bomvu wind blows,
Picks up all luhlata stuff from the ground
Trees are luhlata, people are dark sundvu.

Oh, what a lovely luhlata car.
Running like a bomvu cat with luhlata eyes.
I saw a mnyama spotty snake crawling right behind
    the mthubi, luhlata, bomvu car.
I saw a mnyama girl as pretty as a bomvu rose
    driving the car.

The students of St. Mary's Secondary School

Author and Title Index
of Adult Poems

This index lists the adult poems in the book according to certain themes and forms. Different readers, of course, may find different connections. Related poems are sometimes good to read to children along with their own poems at the end of a lesson or to help inspire them before they write.

About the Author

KENNETH KOCH'S books of poetry include *The Pleasures of Peace, Thank You,* and *Ko, or A Season on Earth.* He is the author of *Wishes, Lies and Dreams: Teaching Children to Write Poetry* and *A Change of Hearts: Plays, Films and Other Dramatic Works.* He lives in New York City and teaches at Columbia University.